Praise for *The Value c*

Aging is challenging. As the number of candles on my birthday cake increases to the size of a bonfire, and the woman I see in the mirror reflects my advancing years, I hope to be treated with the respect Isabel Tom gives her aging charges. *The Value of Wrinkles* is an encouraging look at how we can honor and respect those who are in the final third of their lives. Her stories of Mama and Yeye are heartwarming and real. This isn't a boring how-to book, but rather a story of how the elderly can enrich our lives.

JANE DALY | Author of *The Caregiving Season: Finding Grace to Honor Your Aging Parent* and *Because of Grace: A Mother's Journey from Grief to Hope*

The Value of Wrinkles is a welcome cultural corrective for our youth-obsessed society. Isabel shows us how friendships dissolve the confines of loneliness and depression to brighten the lives of young and old alike.

IRA BYOCK, MD | Author of *Dying Well* and *The Best Care Possible;* founder of the Institute for Human Caring, Providence St. Joseph Health

If you struggle with how to love the older person in your life, *The Value of Wrinkles* is the perfect place to start. Isabel's words are fun, convicting, and practical all at the same time. Recommended reading for grandchildren and adult children alike.

AMANDA GILL | Executive Director at Arbor Terrace Fulton

What a refreshing and compassionate look at the dignity of being old. *The Value of Wrinkles* brilliantly exposes the stereotypical bias of ageism that dominates our current culture. Very well done and a worthwhile read.

JOHN C. ERICKSON | Founder of Erickson Living

So as not to have the regret "not having spent enough time with" or "not having said the things I should have" to your loving elders, read this book and follow the practical, heartfelt advice. A beautifully written, precise account from personal experiences with a humbling approach. A delight to read and a must for everyone.

SHAHID AZIZ, MD, FAAP | Author, *Courageous Conversations on Dying: The Gift of Palliative Care*

Sometimes we have to admit to ourselves we don't know everything. And this is especially true with aging since most of us haven't gotten there yet. Isabel's book is a powerful reminder that we all can benefit from having an older person in our lives.

GEOFF COLEMAN, MD, MHA | Chief Medical Officer at Montgomery Hospice

With her unique perspective as a young professional with an "old soul," Isabel Tom shares her wisdom about aging persons and helps the reader see clearly how their strengths and challenges can be the foundation for mutually rewarding intergenerational relationships. Her practical guide combines an interdisciplinary approach with a deeply spiritual love of the aging to describe a world I want to grow old in.

JUDAH L. RONCH, PhD | Professor and former dean, The Erickson School, UMBC; coeditor, *Culture Change in Elder Care* and *Models and Pathways for Person Centered Elder Care*

The author is very astute in making connections between the stories she tells about living with older grandparents and the ways that we can gain new perspectives and strengthen our relationships with the older adults in our lives. I can see *The Value of Wrinkles* being useful for healthcare professionals and those who serve older adults as they try to examine their own thoughts and feelings about aging. I can also see how it could help medical and nursing students who may be working with older adults in clinical settings to be more aware of the wisdom, humor, and relationship that older adults continue to offer to those who listen. This book would be a useful companion for courses specific to aging, whether in social science, healthcare, or other related fields.

BEVERLY K. LUNSFORD, PhD, RN, FAAN | Assistant Professor at GW School of Nursing ; codirector of the GW Center for Aging, Health and Humanities

Heartwarming, honest, and very compelling. A great read and one that reminds me throughout why some of us have committed our careers to the service of elders. I would say that elders are the largest repository of accumulated wisdom—in the form of walking, talking people—that is currently available to us in the world.

KEVIN D. HEFFNER, MAGS | President of LifeSpan Network

A must-read book for every millennial (or I might say every person under the age of 40). This book beautifully celebrates our elderly with dignity and respect. It is funny, honest, heartfelt, and most of all, honors a generation that has given us all we are proud of in this country.

ROBERT VAN DYK | President/CEO, Van Dyk Health Care

Isabel has a unique, infectious, and compassionate perspective on growing older. *The Value of Wrinkles* has left me awestruck! She has this incredible ability to leave the reader at peace with gaining wrinkles, serving those with wrinkles, and tapping into the older community as an essential source of experience and wisdom. Our society needs more people like Isabel Tom.

LINNÉA BYERS, 35

This book brings to life some beautiful insights into how we can care for and interact with our older adult community. Isabel's personal stories are super relatable and made it very easy to read!

CRYSTAL MAK, 24

The Value of Wrinkles challenged me to see older relatives not just as people you "have to" visit but as treasure troves of wisdom and stories. This book tugged at my heart strings as it brought back tender memories of my grandparents. I wish I read this book while they were still around so I could have made more of the time I had with them.

ANGELO CAPILI, 44

THE
VALUE
OF
WRINKLES

a young perspective
on how loving the old
will change your life

isabel tom

NORTHFIELD PUBLISHING

CHICAGO

Edited by Amanda Cleary Eastep
Interior Design: Erik M. Peterson
Cover Design: Kelsey Fehlberg
Author Photo: Tung Tu Photography

All websites and phone numbers listed herein are accurate at the time of publication but may change in the future or cease to exist. The listing of website references and resources does not imply publisher endorsement of the site's entire contents. Groups and organizations are listed for informational purposes, and listing does not imply publisher endorsement of their activities.

Library of Congress Cataloging-in-Publication Data

Names: Tom, Isabel, author.
Title: The value of wrinkles : a young perspective on how loving the old will change your life / Isabel Tom.
Description: Chicago : Northfield Publishers, [2020] | Includes bibliographical references. | Summary: "What we miss out on when we overvalue youth We're so afraid of aging that we begin to devalue ourselves and others with each passing year. The phrase "30 years old" incites panic. Seniors live in separate communities with little interaction with young people, and middle-aged people spend millions each year on anti-aging products. But what if we have it all wrong? Isabel Tom grew up living with grandparents and has spent over a decade of her career in end-of-life care. Today she: --teaches you what the elderly offer us that we cannot live without --challenges our cultural beliefs and practices that affect those who are aging --gives you practical insight on how to care for those older than you Plus, the book includes a section written from senior citizens entitled, "I Wish You Knew . . ." Age isn't a curse, and the elderly among us deserve better. Will you be a part of the change?"-- Provided by publisher.
Identifiers: LCCN 2019040258 (print) | LCCN 2019040259 (ebook) | ISBN 9780802419538 | ISBN 9780802498168 (ebook)
Subjects: LCSH: Older people. | Old age. | Aging.
Classification: LCC HQ1061 .T656 2020 (print) | LCC HQ1061 (ebook) | DDC 305.26--dc23
LC record available at https://lccn.loc.gov/2019040258
LC ebook record available at https://lccn.loc.gov/2019040259

We hope you enjoy this book from Northfield Publishing. Our goal is to provide high-quality, though-provoking books and products that connect truth to your real needs and challenges. For more information on other books and products that will help you with all your important relationships, go to www.moodypublishers.com or write to:

Northfield Publishers
820 N. LaSalle Boulevard
Chicago, IL 60610

1 3 5 7 9 10 8 6 4 2

Printed in the United States of America

In memory of my dad, Samuel To

Because I have breath, I write. I miss you
and I love you.

And to Mama and Yeye, my two favorite elders.

CONTENTS

DON'T MISS OUT

Tap, tap, tap. It was December and I must have been six or seven. With eyes shut, breathing deeply, I sat at my desk tapping pencil to forehead as I wrestled over one question: What should I give my grandparents for Christmas? Tap, tap, tap. The walls seemed to lean in waiting for an answer. My stuffed animals stared in anticipation. But I had nothing. I dropped my pencil and sighed. There was no use being creative. Rather than racking my brain for more ideas, I thought, why not just ask them?

Luckily, I didn't have far to go. My bedroom, which I shared with my two older sisters, sat on the top floor in our house. Conveniently, the bedroom next door was occupied by my grandparents. Mama, which means "paternal grandmother," and Yeye, which means "paternal grandfather" in Cantonese, emigrated from Hong Kong to the States after my parents invited my grandparents to live with them. By the time I arrived, Mama was 68; Yeye was 71. I wasn't taking notes about the elderly then. I wouldn't have even considered my grandparents old. I simply sat on their laps, snuggled with them, and toddled behind holding their hand as they walked me to school year after year. We started with baby steps. Ended with walkers. Simply, we grew old together.

That afternoon, as Yeye rested in his oversized recliner and Mama browsed the Chinese newspaper in that hard wooden school chair, I bounced into their room, a grin spread across my face. I was ready to solve my holiday dilemma. Gripping my hands together, I asked them, *Nei sing daan zit yiu mat yeh ah?* "What do you want for Christmas?"

"Nuht ding!" Mama cried in her Chinese accent. Seeing my shoulders sag, Mama quickly added, "An orange . . . and a kiss! I don't need anything else!" Yeye chuckled, looked at me, and then nodded in agreement.

Before I knew it, Christmas came and it was time to open presents. I presented Mama with her gift, and she peeled off the layers of tape crisscrossed around the object. The orange skin peeked out, and I immediately planted a giant kiss on her cheek. Mama laughed so hard she was gasping for breath. Then Yeye unwrapped the bar of chocolate I gave him, and I instantly planted a kiss on his cheek as well. He joined in with Mama's laughter.

Almost every Christmas after, I gifted Mama with an orange, Yeye with a chocolate bar, and you better believe, I never forgot the kiss.

Because of sweet moments like this, it may not surprise you to hear that fresh out of college, at age 21, I started my first "real" job at a local retirement community. Now in my mid-thirties, serving the older generation isn't just a job, it's become a career—one in which I've spent over a decade working in almost every level of senior care, including independent living, assisted living, nursing and rehab, and end-of-life. Ironically, the population I served declined progressively with each job. And with each new role, I noticed my grandparents decline at the same rate. It was humbling to say the least. As I encouraged older adults to stay fit, I watched as my grandparents were physically active at home. As I prepared handouts for a seminar about the signs and symptoms of someone nearing death, I spotted the very same symptoms in my grandparents.

People are always intrigued when they hear that I work with the old. People are even more intrigued when they hear that I love it. It's true. I do in fact *love* old people. I'm fascinated by them. Take notice of them. Lean in when they share a word. And as a bystander, I watch and secretly wish to be their friend. Not in the greedy I-want-your-money kind of way. But in the you-are-so-amazing-let-me-hear-your-story-and-get-an-autograph type of way.

Believe me when I tell you, however, that though I grew up living with my grandparents, I didn't always appreciate them. In high school, I walked home every day, and every afternoon without fail, Mama and Yeye sat at our living room window staring down the street as they awaited my arrival—I was the highlight of their day. The moment they recognized my speck from a block away, the front door swung open. Instantly, I knew I was no longer alone.

This was my life. I was *adored*. It was seemingly good, yet frustratingly different.

I loved my grandparents, but as time went on, I wanted out. I was tired of being smothered with attention. In Chinese culture, however, moving out on your own is not customary. To properly do so, you need a ring on your finger, and you need to have said your "I do's."

At the time, I wasn't willing to grab any young buck off the road. So after graduating college, I became one of those kids who moved back in with their parents. Unfortunately, my middle sister left for grad school, and my oldest sister had already married and moved out. That meant I was the only child left at home, perhaps the most dreaded position for a post-college grad. To be the only child and grandchild to nag? Good grief! All worry and attention would trickle down to me; I wasn't sure how I would manage.

Around the same time, I started dating a guy named Kevin (who later became my husband). He was handsome, athletic, and outdoorsy. In our dating days, Kevin hung out at our home often. On one occasion, we drove on a daytrip from Maryland to New Jersey for a wedding. After a long, late-night drive, we pulled quietly into our driveway. It was about two in the morning, and we were exhausted and relieved to be home.

As Kevin's car slowly came to a halt, I remember a blazing fog light (one that should never be sold to the general public) interrupted the stillness of the night. It glared down from the third-floor window of my house. Until then, I had forgotten Yeye owned such a gigantic "flashlight." As it scanned back and forth across the front lawn, it illuminated Kevin's car, as if to say, "Aha! I found you!"

We squinted up at the window, the light shut off, and within seconds the front door opened. Holding his black goat-hair overcoat across his bony body, Yeye nonchalantly appeared at the door, just like the secret service. With his endearing smile, Yeye welcomed me in as he waved Kevin goodbye. Yeye had just happened to be heading to the bathroom. At least that's what he said.

I'm not sure what your grandparent experience was like, but having lived with them for the first twenty-six years of my life, I felt smothered and stuck. Stuck in what I equate to a really long internship: a live-in opportunity with my grandparents. Naturally, I would have preferred to stay at the internship I had at the mall. After all, that was only 9 to 5. But God had other plans. He gave me a 24-hour gig with Mama and Yeye and kept me in-house. All so I could watch, feel, and live alongside two special people as they aged.

Through having grandparents as long-term housemates, something special happened: at a young age, I acquired two very old friends. I also gained an inside perspective on the life of an older person. Without having to need dentures. Without having to use a walker. Without even developing a full head of white hair!

If not for that inside perspective, my passion to serve the older generation would never have developed. If not for that inside perspective I would never have discovered just how valuable older people are.

In addition, working professionally serving older adults has been an eye-opening journey. I learned how to respect elders in various ways and in a different setting. Rather than saying, "Hey old man!" I was trained to greet the elderly cheerfully by name: "Good morning, Mr. Smith!" or "Good morning, El-oise." That simple greeting helped me feel more comfortable around older people other than my grandparents.

I had only used the term "grandparent" before, but over time I became acquainted with other terms used in the aging industry. For example, "older adult," "elder," and "senior" are all used to describe someone 65 and up. As I adopted these terms used in the aging field, I discovered something surprising—even when I used the most politically correct terms, some older people were still offended. As a 20-, 30-, or 40-something, you may wonder: How should I address someone who is in their sixties, seventies, eighties, and beyond?

No perfect term exists. But I learned that no matter what term you use, every older adult will welcome a certain dispo-sition—one of respect, honor, and gratitude. Thus, in the fol-lowing chapters I will use terms like "the old," "older people," and "older adults." Initially, it may trigger a negative response because "old" is often considered derogatory. My intention throughout, however, is to show that the term "old," and even being old, is not shameful; rather, old age is honorable and something to be proud of.

Because of the knowledge I've acquired over the years about aging, my career experience (as happens with many health professionals) set me on hyperalert anytime something happened to my grandparents. When Mama fell a little over a year ago, I immediately understood the signs and risks. Falls often indicate a person's body is weakening. Falls can also be the beginning of a downward spiral in an older adult's health. In only a day, Mama wasn't able to do things she previously could. She needed help to stand up. She couldn't walk on her own, even a few steps. She sat and slept increasingly more.

Within a week, as Mama grew dramatically weaker, our family quickly realized that our efforts to care for Mama's needs were unsustainable. We made the hard decision to move her to a nursing home. If you've been in this situation, you know this is a cry-your-eyes-out type of experience. It makes you feel overwhelmingly guilty. Yet one thing brought me comfort, and it was that my husband and I lived right down the street. And so, for many a night, after my three little ones (5 and under) were tucked away and the nursing home front desk had already closed down, I made my way back to Room 180, sometimes for a second or third time that day. I did not want Mama, even for a minute, to feel alone. I wanted her to know she was loved. I wanted her to know she had not been abandoned.

In the beginning of 2018, I reluctantly retired my grandchild title, as Mama, at 102, took her final breath. I had grown up on Mama, literally, having sat on her lap so many times.

I miss her dearly, yet her goodbye was perfect in a special way; even the nursing home staff admitted to that. In her last years, a village had come together to shower Mama with love. We spoiled her to the very end. Truthfully, it was hard work. It required sacrifice, complicated scheduling, being on-call, overnight stays, energy, and of course, patience. But I was so glad I was part of that.

Because as I poured out my heart, energy, and time to love on Mama, I found myself better because of it. Throughout my life, Mama, Yeye, and hundreds of older men and women have blessed me in ways I never expected an "old person" to. They've inspired me. Given me the straight answer. Reminded me not to give up. Told me I have a gift. They've shared golden insight. They've calmed my heart. They've taught me true beauty. They have shined so much light into my life. Outwardly, my service may have appeared sacrificial at times, but it really came down to this—when I served my grandma, I gained something from it.

This book is all about the journey of how I went from grumbling about my grandparents to being grateful for them. Because I don't want you to miss out on seeing the value of wrinkles. As someone in your twenties, thirties, or forties, it is so easy to be wrapped up in the busy day-to-day of our lives. Through this book, my hope is to stop you in your frenzied life and to remind you of the blessing of having white-haired citizens in our midst. Seeking and cultivating a relationship with an older person is a worthwhile use of your time. This will have a profound impact on your life—and on theirs. When you finish *The Value of Wrinkles*, you will know practical ways that you—as a grandchild, adult child, or simply a younger friend—can connect with, bless, and encourage the older person in your life. You will feel empowered and equipped to love them better.

I will warn you, this book is not a manual containing the intricate details of senior care. Rather, this is a book aimed at improving our attitudes and our heart toward our elders. You see, before we look into the type of care an elder needs, we first need to assess whether we have the right attitude and heart to give it. For good care is only good when it is given with love.

So let's get to it. Because this is a generation that for so long has been underestimated, undervalued, and forgotten. Each wrinkled face deserves so much more.

Here's my salute to the older generation.

chapter 1

THAT WASN'T A WHITE HAIR, WAS IT?

What do you do when a white hair appears? I have black hair, and when a white one sneaks in, it is *extremely* noticeable. A disadvantage of being short and Asian. A year ago, I posted the same question to Facebook friends. "What do you do when a white hair appears?" Oh, the responses.

The majority get rid of them. Some pluck. Some shave their heads bald. Others wait impatiently until the next round of dye. Finally, some refuse to pluck for fear of having two more grow in its place. Honestly, if I glance in the mirror and discover another white strand, I privately freak out. *What is this? Another one?!* Then I pluck that sucker out!

Tell me if you can relate. In my early twenties, I felt hopeful for life. By 25, I was still trucking along quite fine. But as I inched closer to that thirtieth birthday, I panicked. And proactively, I handled my fear by doing two things.

First, I decided to deliver my first kid before my twenty-ninth birthday. With a breech baby, the doctor allowed me to choose the day of my C-section. I chose a Tuesday, three days *before* my twenty-ninth birthday. That way it'd go down in the books that I delivered my first baby at 28—it just sounded better.

Next, when the big 3-0 rolled around, I went for a new look. My hairstylist friend offered to give me highlights, so I drove two hours to her salon and invited a new color into my life. Doing something new seemed like the best way to ring in the next decade.

I'm fairly sure I'm not the only who has suffered an early midlife crisis. Every day, I overhear conversations or swipe through social media posts noticing that almost *all* of us are worrying or thinking about aging, to some degree. Have you ever cringed when someone asked how old you are? Or posted on social media how you're getting "up there" in age? Have you ever shied away from celebrating your own birthday?

Countless numbers of people are panicking over old age—to the point that businesses and entire industries, fully aware of our insecurity, are making money off of this. See for yourself: visit any beauty products website and type in the term "anti-aging." When I searched one popular site, over 1,700 anti-aging products appeared. All products trying to combat the terrifying process of aging. Deep down, we're afraid that the older we get, the less capable, less attractive, and less valuable we become.

*"I get my hair dyed—dark brown recently.
I have highlights and get so many compliments; it
makes me look younger."*

TERRY, 85

Subtly, this deep-seeded anxiety has seeped into the way we approach the older generation, which in this book I define as someone 65 years old and up (simply because this is how most well-developed countries have defined it).[1] Whatever your definition of age, have you ever considered how our fear of aging can have a destructive impact?

WHAT OUR ROAD RAGE REVEALS

I'm already ten minutes late for work, but the cool breeze rushes through the window, a wakeup call for a late morning. The radio blares my favorite song. All. Is. Well. But as I pull onto Main Street, about to accelerate, I jolt to a halt. I can't believe it. There I am, stuck trudging behind a slow-moving car. A second later, I peel out from behind the car and into the left lane. "Finally!" As I speed past and glance out my right window, I see two bony hands gripping the steering wheel. Clearly a white-haired citizen. "Should have figured," I mutter.

Over the years, I've discovered this type of road rage is no isolated case. If you were in the passenger seat, you'd probably think nothing of it.

Jump into my car for a minute. Here we are again behind another slow-moving car. Can you believe it? This time around, rather than griping about a white-haired citizen, imagine I'm complaining about the color, gender, sexuality, or the immigration status of this driver turtling along.

Red flags are flying everywhere. You might have thrown out a few of your own. I said something wrong, didn't I? Were you offended by my rude behavior? Put off a bit? Perhaps I owe some apologies.

In a time when our society is increasingly sensitive toward racism, sexism, and other social injustices, isn't it odd we are so at ease with belittling the older generation? Our sensitivity is selective.

Crippled old man. Slow old driver. Grumpy old neighbor. Difficult elderly family members.

Let's admit it. We all know the nine o'clock news prefers a younger face. Once a sliver of white appears, that TV anchor may soon be on her way out. In the producer's mind, the anchor needs to be replaced by younger talent, half her age, unless the anchor dyes her hair and injects some doses of Botox. No surprise. You and I know how it works. And really, I completely understand. Young and new does sound better.

When I hear someone under 65 declare, "I'm getting old!" my nostrils start twitching. My

> In a time when our society is increasingly sensitive toward racism, sexism, and other social injustices, isn't it odd we are so at ease with belittling the older generation? Our sensitivity is selective.

jaw clenches. Deep breathing exercises automatically kick in. Look around—not a fiber in people's bones are ignited. Not even an eyebrow is raised. Life goes on. And on and on. No heated debate on social media erupts. Nothing goes viral. No polite "excuse me" is said. People even laugh.

Laughing happens when there's a good joke. But it also happens when someone wants to avoid further embarrassment. They laugh with others now, only to cry about it later.

Hang out with enough older people, and some will say, "You don't want to hang out with an old guy like me!" There he is, laughing it off. Not in the humorous, healing type of way. But in a shameful way.

"Old age? I didn't know there was any good left in it."

BILL, 82

When diminished, ignored, misunderstood, and undervalued, our older citizens are laughing along. Shame has displaced the honor of old age.

Therefore, when we see hallways full of older faces looking as if life has been sucked out of them, why then are we surprised? Why are we surprised when older people feel guilty for asking for help or withhold health issues from us? Why are we surprised when we see a grandparent or older parent attempting unsafe tasks on their own? At the heart of it, society has led our older citizens to believe they are worthless. We have led them to believe they are in the way. Useless. Instead of acknowledging their age, people have become ashamed of it.

SERVING THE YOUNG SOUNDS BETTER

In my twenties, a good friend once commented how she was intrigued by my career choice. She wasn't fond of older people; she also genuinely didn't understand why people would choose to serve them.

Instead of serving older adults, my friend worked with children. After all, working with children seems like a more worthwhile endeavor because our future depends on the youth. Why serve "old people" when they will die within a matter of time?

Isn't it interesting how we begin to devalue people? When someone is young, we are eager to serve because they are the future. A toddler is precious at age two, and as he or she enters kindergarten, they bubble with promise. Fast forward decades later. Ironically, when that same child turns 82, we stick them in a recliner in the corner, overlook their achievements, tell them to play Bingo, and quietly transfer love and admiration to someone younger, someone "more worth our time." We love young faces, but when that young face develops wrinkles, we couldn't care less for them. It's so natural we don't even think about it.

The Issue Is Big

Our negative perceptions toward aging aren't confined to our minds or even to the walls of our home. Our negative views poison the individuals around us, and they can even endanger the entire older adult population. In 2018, older adults accounted for sixteen percent of the population, an estimated

52.3 million people.[2] By 2040, that number is projected to jump to 82.3 million older adults.[3] In no time, not only will we be surrounded by older adults, you and I will be caring for them too (you may already be doing this). What we believe about aging has the potential to cripple millions of older souls. And that can impact our economy, our healthcare system, our neighborhoods, and even the minute-to-minute of our lives. That's why *this* is the time to address our views of the older generation. *This* is the time to learn how to treat them well. This is the time to learn how to honor them. Not simply because it impacts their lives, but because it impacts ours too.

Where the Mix-Up Occurs

The potential for decline and the changing of our bodies is a reality of aging. There can be wrinkles and walkers. Aches. Daily pains. Even hourly ones. A knee replacement, sometimes followed by another knee replacement. Weak eyes. Loss of hearing. The disabling fall. And then repeated ones. Infections. Hospital visits. In-home help. Then comes the trauma of being moved out of your home. And I hate to say it but, yes, sometimes diapers.

Here is where we have it all wrong. We associate decline in health with decline in value. As our minds naturally zero in on the harsh realities of aging, we need to remember that though our bodies are failing, our worth is not waning. Aging involves goodness too. Being older means we are living longer. And living longer means we have been blessed with more time with family and friends. Living longer means we are able to gain wisdom and experience. Living longer means we can gain maturity and depth. These are all valuable qualities in a person. Yet, often we don't see them. This is how we end up with an unbalanced view of aging.

....

A year ago, I was visiting an elderly man at an assisted living facility; he was nearing the end of his life. A hospice nurse had come to check on him. As we sat beside him, the man mouthed words but couldn't speak.

"What do you want to tell us?" the nurse asked.

With chairs pulled up close and ears ready to listen, the nurse and I waited for him to speak. His voice was faint. His words were completely garbled. We couldn't understand.

At times, we literally can't hear the old. We simply can't decipher their words. If we're being honest, however, other times we have no ears to hear. We're not available. Maybe we're simply not willing. Therefore, we often lose sight of the needs of the older generation.

With vulnerable populations, there are often people who speak up and advocate for them. Survivors or caregivers tell their story and give voice to their needs.

When it comes to the older generation, sadly, few are speaking up and advocating for them. Few people are telling their story or giving voice to their needs. There's good reason for this: when it comes to aging, there are *no* survivors. A wife cares for her seriously ill husband aware that her time is soon to come. She has no energy to advocate.

This is why the older generation is often not on our radar.

WHAT IS TRUE?

Finally, brothers and sisters, whatever is true, whatever is noble, whatever is right, whatever is pure, whatever is lovely, whatever is admirable—if anything is excellent or praiseworthy—think about such things.
(Phil. 4:8)

Having attended church since childhood, I heard this verse about a million times. Yet I only remembered one phrase: Think about what is lovely.

This made good sense to me. I loved thinking about flowers, my future wedding, and marshmallow clouds. Loads of gummy candy. Beaches with warm sun and breezes. Yet it wasn't until I became an adult that I finally noticed the other "whatevers" in this verse, like: "whatever is true." For the longest time, I didn't understand what this meant. Then one day I had an "aha" moment: I should rest my thoughts on flowers, but I also should rest my thoughts on reality.

> *"You have to be realistic about life.*
> *You know you come into the world as a baby,*
> *you grow up as a child, as an adult, and then,*
> *a seasoned adult."*
>
> **MARY, 85**

It's hard to believe thinking can solve anything. But I believe the Holy Word has merit in what it says. We can't send every plate of leftover dinner to children in poverty, but when we are aware of the current condition in any part of our world, it makes a difference.

To think about "whatever is true" is to face our own fears of aging. But it also means reaching out to understand someone's reality. When we seek to know someone's situation, we don't offer solutions. We simply listen.

When we listen, we become more compassionate people. We learn what poverty feels like. We uncover the pain of depression. We experience a glimpse of abandonment. We shudder over the horror of abuse. When we listen, we look into someone else's life and seek to understand a part of their reality.

And that's the crux of it. As a society, we have a poor understanding of the older person. We have focused on the end of an older person's story, rather than on their whole life. We have relied on media's portrayals to depict what elders are like. We have depended on a few interactions, however meaningful, with older people. Maybe that's why we go kicking and screaming as we're dragged into the next decade. We haven't seen the real deal of aging. To uncover the best qualities of older adults, we need real-life encounters.

So, the next time you cringe when you have to honestly fill out your age on a form or hit a birthday and feel that panic attack coming on, here's a tip: look for an elder and figure out "whatever is true" in their life. Invite Grandpa, Grandma, Mom, Dad, or an older friend to coffee, take them to a baseball game, or simply visit them. Then ask how *they* survived their 30th or 40th birthday. Listen. Let them share their story. Hear them out, and gain a picture of what real old age is like.

It will ease your fears; it will give both of you a good laugh.

To see the value of wrinkles, this is a good place to start.

chapter 2

I'VE GOT TIME
FOR YOU

With glasses at age two, I started off on the wrong fashion foot. As a young child, my signature hairstyle was a short, poofy, overgrown bush, and to complete the "look," I consistently sported sweat pants and hand-me-downs.

In elementary school, a kid on the playground asked me if I was a boy or a girl. In middle school, a well-meaning friend hinted, "You should grow out your hair and get contacts." Boys did not have crushes on girls like me.

By ninth grade, although I had grown out my hair and dropped the thick lenses, like any teenage girl, I still wanted to fit in. I yearned for straight, shiny black hair. Cute brand-name clothes. And secretly I dreamed of hearing my classmates had voted *me* to be Homecoming Princess.

Awkward stages, especially drawn-out ones, can affect our sense of self-worth for life. Maybe you had some super lively bangs or flashy braces. Maybe you were "too fat" or "too skinny." The hurt experienced in these stages can cause one to seek out unhealthy attention and cause confidence to spiral; these experiences can even drive a person into deep depression. Without a doubt, I had moments where I hid under the sheets and cried my eyes out. But oddly, I didn't stay there.

BOUNCING BACK

In fact, despite my dorky appearance and failures, I maintained a surprisingly happy and cheerful demeanor. When I started college, I was confident to make new friends. I desired to try new things. I dreamt of future endeavors.

As I think back to childhood, I see that over time, I developed a resilience to bounce back despite rejection. And it had so much to do with the fact that I had grandparents who had time for me. The time, attention, and availability that older adults can offer are valuable assets to society. Their time can help us build resilience for adversity, which is especially valuable in adolescence. Mama and Yeye's time was one of the best gifts they offered me (almost as good as the oranges and chocolate bars I gave them). And it wasn't that my parents didn't love me (because they surely did), it was that my grandparents provided me an extra layer of love and attention. They had the time to shower it on me and to give me a continual and abundant supply of it.

A Safe Place

In my freshman year, I joined the nursing home ministry at my school (probably because I missed being around my grandparents). Stepping into a nursing home was, to say the least, uncomfortable. Looking down the hallways, you could see people sitting in lines of wheelchairs with their heads hung down. Other elderly residents just sat in their rooms staring off into the distance. Televisions blared, unwatched. Conversation was rare.

Even though it was uncomfortable at first, I came to really appreciate the setting of a nursing home. It wasn't the typical place for a college student to make friends, but over the next four years, there were two residents in particular that I befriended: Burt and Elsie.

Burt was bedridden. His eyes evidenced he was completely aware, but his mouth could barely form a sentence. When I walked into his room, he always lay in bed with white sheets covering him, just as if he was in the hospital. In the beginning, I didn't know what to say. How could I make conversation with someone who could barely talk? But week after week, even if I only had few words or I made up things to share, Burt always seemed pleased to see me. I'm unsure how, but he always had a fresh stash of chocolate. At the end of every visit, he'd always instruct me to open the bottom drawer of his dresser and take a piece of chocolate to go. I still remember on Valentine's Day, when secret admirers were nowhere to be found, Burt had a chocolate heart waiting for me.

Elsie, my other friend, had glasses that looked outdated

and dark brown hair that flailed in every direction. Early on, I noticed one of her shoes had a sole almost three inches thicker than the other. One of her legs was significantly longer than the other: that frightened me at first. But I kept visiting. Each week, when I walked into her room, Elsie would pop up from a nap, and then scoot to the edge of the bed.

She never had much to say, which made it awkward at first. But in time, I learned how to make conversation with Elsie, a woman I knew nothing about. Sometimes I would stumble trying to figure out what to say next. And then I'd try again. But Elsie didn't flinch. She just laughed.

In hindsight, I see that it was in the nursing home setting, with people like Burt and Elsie, where I learned to interact with people very different than myself. Interestingly, this helped me thrive once I entered a professional setting. *Harvard Business Review* reports that one of the biggest challenges recent graduates face when transitioning from college to the professional workforce is building relationships strategically, which involves "interacting regularly with people of different ages, backgrounds and interests."[1] Burt and Elsie were always happy to see me; they were available. And they provided me with a safe environment to develop skills that would benefit me for a lifetime.

Dependable

In a time of life when relationships and the future can be iffy, Burt and Elsie became dependable friends of mine. During my field hockey season, I was unable to visit the nursing home with the college's group at their scheduled time. So I started visiting Burt and Elsie on my own because I knew they were available any time. We didn't have to search our calendars for an open day; they didn't rush off to another appointment. They were available and dependable: I liked that.

The sad truth is, as nursing home residents, Burt and Elsie didn't have the freedom to leave and engage in activities outside the building. Their lack of independence is why they were always available. Yet the availability of older folks, even the bedridden ones, is what makes them some of the most dependable friends. Your first instinct may be to roll your eyeballs because surely someone who is bedridden has nothing to offer. In chapter 11, you'll see how I discovered this is far from the truth.

The availability of older adults is something we can all gain from. Because even loving parents and siblings who become the best of friends can be too busy for us. Parents work. Siblings move away. Peers start dating, have families, and are gone for seasons. Neighbors rush in and out of their homes. Yet when others are too busy, older folks . . . they're there.

Even when I was newly married (officially labelled as "never lonely"), I found times when I'd be out running errands and wanted to talk to someone. Mama, then in her nineties, was my favorite person to call; she was reliably home:

"Hi, Ma. What are you doing?"

"Oh, just sitting around like a mooncake."

Our conversations were brief, yet I appreciated having a friend to check in with. One I could call at any time. One I could call for absolutely no reason at all. Mama was my go-to-girlfriend. And that happened because she was always there.

DO I HAVE YOUR ATTENTION?

Along with being available, I so appreciate how older people are also then able to give us undivided attention. In a time when conversations are always interrupted and eye contact is even hard to win, this is a rare commodity. When someone gives us their undivided attention, they communicate a strong message that we matter.

As a parent, I know the importance of spending one-on-one time with my children and giving them my undivided attention. But when it comes down to it, scheduling dates with all three of them, not to mention my husband, and determining the order of who goes first is like a triple-action calculus problem. It is painful to solve.

For those of you who are parents, you are well aware that on a daily basis, our kids are pushing each other for a space on our laps, fighting over who will sit next to us at dinner, and constantly interrupting each other, upping their volume so we can hear *their* story. Even when it seems like we're in the clear and could possibly sit down to read a book to one of the kids, we're thrown into the hamster wheel again. Someone else needs us!

The times we have to tell someone "wait a sec," "hold on," or "not right now" can outnumber the "I love yous," and "What is it, sweetiepies?" But a blowout diaper, a sticky spill, or a boo-boo is not something that can wait. The flow of dirty dishes and laundry will continue to stream. We want to give attention to everyone in the family, but yesterday, today, and tomorrow, we'll be occupied.

This is where older adults are so valuable. While not every

grandparent is healthy enough to help with childcare, all grandparents can help give our children more attention, and remind them that they matter. Sure, grandparents may get our instructions wrong at times. They may bend the rules even. But they possess a strength to fill in the gaps. Between exhaustion and limitation of time for our kids, older adults and especially grandparents can nurture our kids. They can shower them with admiration and undivided attention. They don't replace parents, but they give us grace (and sometimes much-needed rest) to keep on going.

So before you think to shoo off the grandparents for messing up your kids' schedules or feeding them something too sweet for breakfast, remember how precious their presence is. Grandpa can read a story to a child and be fully present. Grandma can sit and watch an entire television show without having to be interrupted. An older neighbor can engage in a conversation and listen with adoration. With their time, older adults have the ability to give us an extra layer of love: to affirm us, to nurture us, and to cushion us with love for the hard blows in life. Children or not, we all yearn and appreciate the undivided attention of others. It reminds us we matter.

THEY TAKE CARE OF US

Our natural assumption is that we will have to care for the old. Sometimes in spending enough time together, we find they begin taking care of us. I recently met a busy mom of six children. About a decade ago, when her busy family lived in

Maryland, they became quite fond of their seventy-year-old next-door neighbor. They were so fond of her that when they moved to another state, they invited their unmarried neighbor to move with them. She had beloved pets to care for. And frankly, the offer seemed too outrageous; so as you might expect, the neighbor declined.

This family now lives in Minnesota. Since their time in Maryland ten years ago, their beloved neighbor has experienced several health issues. Having kept in touch with her, they again invited her to move in with them. This time she accepted. And so, from Maryland to Minnesota this older woman went.

With six children to care for, this mom already has a lot on her hands. Surely, having another person in the house would increase her load. But when I spoke with this mom, she looked at me and exclaimed: "I thought I was going to have to care for *her*. Well, she cares for *me*. She washes *all* my dishes! When I have guests, she tells them she will wash the dishes. She says, 'I now have a purpose, and it's to help you.'"

> *"My maternal grandma literally is a superhero. She can cook; she takes care of people. She is always very caring and loving toward everyone. Especially the grandkids. She will take time to travel to Virginia, New York, Maryland, and between those places to visit all of us, to stay with us, and care for all of us."*
>
> **KRISTIE, 22**

Sometimes we underestimate older adults and give them seemingly unimportant tasks so they can feel helpful. But often times, older adults have the time and willingness to make a real impact in our lives. They can offer a helping hand, and like this older woman, they can relieve a busy mom-of-six from one of her many jobs. As you go about your day, look around at how older adults are already contributing in simple yet powerful ways. They are one of society's most underutilized assets.

TIME TO ENCOURAGE US

Older adults have more time on their hands. With less frenzy of work and family responsibilities, they have more time to think about the needs of others; they also have more time to cheer us on.

In college, I played on the Houghton College varsity field hockey team. Because of the distance and because of work, on average, my parents were only able to watch one game every season. Though my parents weren't able to watch me, I was still blessed with plenty of support. Almost every game, our team would hear a duck call from the sidelines. That was Mr. Koch, my teammate's dad. He was retired and noticeably older than most other parents. Because he had more time, Mr. Koch was able to drive and watch every match. Over my four seasons, Mr. and Mrs. Koch treated me like their own daughter, and with duck calls, they'd cheer me on. At the end of every game, both Mr. and Mrs. Koch, like proud parents, would not only pat their daughter's back, they would pat mine too. I was so blessed.

In a time when the busyness of life can leave us feeling forgotten, older adults can acknowledge and remember others in many meaningful ways. This last Valentine's Day, I was at a local retirement community and greeted some elders in the elevator. "Happy Valentine's Day!" I said to them. One of the ladies, who I later found out was 96, told me she forgot it was Valentine's Day. A second later, she leaned over her walker and said to her friend, "Later today I am going to call friends I know who are feeling lonely!" Less distracted, countless seniors are using their time to thoughtfully care for others.

MEANING IN THE MINUTES

We can only uncover the benefits of having an older person in our life if we have a relationship with them. Some of you may wonder how to develop that type of relationship. Looking back, my relationship with my grandparents grew not out of elaborate trips, but from the ordinary moments. Come to think of it, Mama and Yeye never sat me down for a heart-to-heart chat. They never took me on dates (they couldn't drive). They didn't treat me to Disney World or the beach. We just spent millions of minutes together.

My time with Mama and Yeye was spent in different ways. Saturday mornings, for example, was a memorable time with Yeye. When we were about 5, 8, and 11, my sisters and I would nibble on our bread as Yeye cooked a hearty breakfast for himself (breakfast was by far his largest meal). He made a giant mug of coffee, a hot dog with lots of ketchup, macaroni salad, and then he'd often cook up some Ramen to go with it. Sitting at the kitchen table, my sisters and I always marveled as Yeye poured the entire pack of seasoning in his noodles; this is something our parents never let us do. As he transferred the pot of noodles to the table, we would sit up on our little knees coming closer to the savory aroma. Ahhh. Yeye would look up, smile, and, pitying our hungry looks, he would ask us if we wanted some. We would cheer. Even if we only got a few strands each, we were still excited and devoured them.

While I bonded over noodles with Yeye, Mama and I bonded over tantrums. With all the "injustices" involved in being the youngest, I flipped out quite often. I remember one instance of many when I was about five, and I was kicking and screaming on the floor. Mama swept me up, and with my tears dripping onto her, she plopped down into her rocking chair. Back and forth she rocked as she patted me gently. Her rocking had a way of calming me. "*Daa pei gu. Ngo mm oi nei le*," she would croon in Cantonese. "I'm going to spank you. I don't love you anymore." But as she rocked and held me tight, I snuggled closer to her warm body because we both knew what she said was far from the truth.

And it was in the millions of minutes that a closeness evolved. This is why bonding with the elderly is so sweet. It requires no budget and little planning. Whether walking, rocking, cleaning, eating, whether changing light bulbs or fixing fences, or eating ice cream or doing nothing together, what matters is the minutes.

The reality, however, is that sometimes we don't have grandparents in the same town, and so these minutes may be harder to come by. Even miles away, a sweet relationship can still develop. It may grow from video chats or random phone calls. It may come in the form of letters or a small souvenir sent after a trip. It can happen by saving up our vacation hours and taking a few days to visit with them. When you make the effort to spend minutes with an older person, you honor them and remind them they matter.

> *"My maternal grandmother and I are actually working on finishing a quilt together that she started way back in the 70s. It is a lot more work than I initially thought!"*
>
> **ALISON, 22**

The harsher reality comes for those of us who don't even have a living grandparent to glean from. While grandparent-grandchild relationships are particularly special, this is not the only way to be blessed by an older person. Quite simply, there are literally millions of older adults in our world we can bless and be blessed by, even if they are not blood related. We can adopt a grandparent at a local senior living facility. We can offer to mow the lawn for a widowed neighbor. We can have lunch with an older coworker or offer a ride to an elderly member of our faith community. We can take the time to chat with an older person at the store.

There are plenty of older people who would appreciate a younger friend. And as we spend ordinary moments together, we can share a laugh, a memory, a disappointment. We come to appreciate their quirks, stories, and wit. In the minutes, we create a welcoming space to hear out the older person's story.

With precious time, older adults have more availability and undivided attention to give. They have time to look out for us and time to encourage us. They bring value to society, more than most people might expect. I've found that older adults want to invest in the lives of those younger than they are. So even if they lead an active life, when they don't *have* time, they often will *make* time for us.

Whether we are struggling with braces, pimples, poofy hair, or overwhelming piles of dishes; whether we are lonely and simply looking for a dependable friend, maybe it's time to reconnect with a grandparent, or another older person. Make a call, pay a visit, and reach out. A precious friendship may be waiting for you.

....

TAKE NOTES | *What Do You Talk to Older Adults About?*

Engaging in conversation with older adults can be awkward or even intimidating for some of us. As you seek to get past the "hellos" with elders you know or meet, here are some basics for better conversations:

USE DIFFERENT QUESTIONS FOR DIFFERENT LIFESTYLES

Asking "How are you?" or "What did you do today?" can sometimes lead to one-word answers, depending on the person and their lifestyle.

An active older adult might have more to say, but a sedentary older adult may not. After I moved out of the house, I would call Mama and ask her what she did that day: ninety-nine percent of the time, she would respond, "Nothing."

When approaching someone who is sedentary, try asking about their preferences such as, "What was your favorite part of lunch today?" or "What type of weather do you like best?" Inquire about activities they are currently engaged in. "I saw you reading the newspaper. What's happening in the world today?"

When approaching the more active older adult, show interest in their day-to-day. "What did you do today?" "What events have you been attending lately?"

Even if the conversation is dry or falls flat, take heart knowing that it is not your conversation but your interest that communicates love.

BRING IN YOUR EXCITING LIFE AND KEEP TALKING

Talking about yourself isn't usually the best rule of thumb, but when trying to engage in meaningful conversation, especially with an older adult, it can be helpful. When we share our lives with an older adult, they often appreciate hearing about our activities and our interests, some of which they may no longer be able to participate in. At times, it may feel like you are the only one talking, but as you tell them about the new restaurants you've tried, your new haircut, your latest discovery, and the new activities you are involved in, you may spark ideas and opinions that lead to deeper conversation.

IGNITE GOOD MEMORIES

Who doesn't love reminiscing over a great memory? Some of the most fun conversations with older adults come when we ask them about the past. When a person is in the earlier stages of Alzheimer's, long-term memories actually tend to stick more than the short-term memories, so bringing up the past can be beneficial.[2] Ask the older person how they passed the time as a child, what kind of school they went to, what it was like to cook back then, or even what type of refrigerator they used (if they even had one). Even better, bring them back to the moment when they first met their spouse. And don't be surprised if you see their eyes light up, and they radiate with delight.

chapter 3

YOUR INVITATION SPEAKS VOLUMES

Have you ever heard someone gushing about a party they're hosting over the weekend, where "this girl," "that girl," and "this guy" are invited? Burgers and hotdogs will be hot off the grill. Ice cream of all flavors will be served. You're giddy with excitement. Your mouth starts salivating. You cannot *wait* to go home and tell your family about it.

But then, you find out you're not invited. Forget the fact that you had another event to attend but canceled already. Sigh . . . in one second, your self-esteem fizzles. It's not that you needed to *attend* the party; you simply wanted to be invited.

The more I work with older people, the more I realize how they too feel excluded at times. Seeing their deflated expressions, I sense how they just wish to be acknowledged. As a society, we have pushed older adults to the outskirts, not only in the figurative sense, but in the literal sense too.

"Our grandchildren are far away and they have their own preoccupations. It would be wonderful to get a note every now and then to say what they're interested in or excited about and ask what we're doing."

WILLIAM, 85

In an ideal world, you could walk into a senior care community and see it bustling with visitors of all ages. From big-eyed babies to toddlers, teenagers, young adults, and adult children too. In the real world, however, the older adults in these places are very much alone. When you walk into their "home," the lobbies and hallways are empty. Every now and then, an adult child comes into the building. They sign in, make their way to their mother's room, and then the lobby quiets again. Until the next visit.

HOME OR SENIOR HOME, WHICH IS BETTER?

Considering the drab environment in some senior living facilities, do you ever think every family should just care for their elder at home? With the high cost of senior care, more adult children are now considering this option. They are buying bigger houses with separate spaces or building in-law suites to offer more privacy. Some are even buying homes in the same neighborhood so that when needed, help is right around the corner.

Sometimes living together is the best arrangement. Lower expenses. In-house childcare. Meeting a family obligation. On the other hand, sometimes living in the same space with another adult is intimidating. We all like things our own way. We like our kitchen organized in a particular fashion. We prefer things completed in a certain order. We set our thermostat at a specific temperature. Inviting someone else into our space essentially opens the door to upset our preferences. A new party changes home life dynamics. A so-called guest shifts our schedules around. Furniture may move. New smells can even evolve.

Balancing our needs with the needs of our elder is no easy task. What's the best living arrangement then? Home? Or senior home? What do you think is the best option?

The Inside Scoop on Intergenerational Living

I am a product of intergenerational living, probably at its best. And I can give you the inside scoop. When it comes to the benefits, there are many. First of all, in living with parents and grandparents, I was blessed to always have a loving adult in the home. Even if my parents were working, Mama and Yeye were there. Primarily, they were my afterschool guardians. They bravely witnessed my first toots on instruments. They watched as my sisters and I DIY-ed our own Halloween costumes. When we created inventions, they marveled at them.

Additionally, in living with grandparents, I gained that extra layer of love, which I mentioned earlier. As the baby of the family, I probably benefited the most. Yeye, with his prickly unshaven face, pecked me with kisses when I came home from school. When I flew up and down the stairs, Mama patted me as I passed by.

As time went on, however, things began to change. My

sisters and I needed less help, and my grandparents needed a little more. This happens in many grandparent-grandchild relationships. Naturally, my sisters and I stepped up and helped however we could. By high school, it wasn't uncommon for Mama to ask for someone to help thread her needle. It wasn't strange for one of us to drive Yeye to the store. In living with elders, my sisters and I learned how to be helpful. We became young players in the caregiving process.

The more my sisters and I helped, the more my grandparents began to depend on us. At the time, I grumbled about this, but in the long run I see it taught me how to serve others, even when it isn't convenient. I found having a grandchild's assistance helped my grandparents feel less of a burden; that lightened their moods. For example, driving Yeye to the grocery store meant a lot to him. Being a powerhouse walker, it was his habit to walk an hour and fifteen minutes six days a week and thus he was strong enough to walk to the store to buy groceries. As he reached his nineties, he still could buy most everything himself, but he couldn't transport the heavier items on his own.

"The things you used to take for granted like getting up and going quickly to another room or whatever. It just doesn't happen. Your head says 'let's go,' and your body says 'come on now.'"

ELIZABETH, 86

Whether in high school or college (and actually even after that), I often would wake up to the sound of Yeye and Mama murmuring and devising how they could get a trip to the store. Through the walls, I could hear Yeye say, "When she wakes up, I'll ask." Once they heard signs that I was awake, they would rush over to my door and knock. With a childlike desperation, Yeye would ask, "Do you think you could take me to the store?"

In living together with Mama and Yeye, my sisters and I developed an awareness of others, especially those who are aging. Mainly because we were front seat and center and could see and hear what my grandparents needed. This is one of the unique advantages of an intergenerational home; children especially become attuned to needs and how they can help.

The Other Side of the Story

Because our family survived decades of living together, people typically assume the intergenerational arrangement in our house was ideal. "You all must have such gentle spirits to be able to do that," someone once commented. Boy, did I chuckle. Because, as usual, there's always another side of the story.

Sadly, the other side of the story starts with trashy talk shows. Growing up, it was practically illegal for my sisters and me to watch television (you could call it a family core value). We first had to ask for permission to watch TV. Then, we also had to ask permission regarding what we watched; Mom and Dad were strict about it. Nothing with swear words. Nothing with kissing. And first homework, piano, chores, and Chinese school homework had to be done. No questions.

Unfortunately, though we had tight restrictions regarding television, in the room next door, a man sat in his recliner watching a boatload of it. He didn't care what the rules were for us kids; he did what he wanted. Thus, when Mom and Dad weren't home, like bees to honey, we were drawn to Yeye's room. We'd stand in the back of the room where he couldn't see us, and if we heard the front door open, we would sprint out of Yeye's room resuming our chores or assignments. And sadly, that's how our young minds were exposed to trashy talk shows, R-rated movies, and daytime soap operas. This is the unfortunate, yet very real, part of living with others.

Other intergenerational households could probably share similar stories. But that large, clunky TV really was a troublemaker in our home. After family dinner, Yeye would head upstairs, and he would flip on the evening news and watch at maximum volume. If anyone asked Yeye to turn it down, he would stand up, turn the dial a smidge, and the TV would continue blaring.

It blared as my sister and I attempted to finish our homework. It blared when my mom dozed off on the couch after a hard day of work. It blared while my dad, a quiet man, tried to read in his study every night. The door of Dad's study was always either completely shut or open but a small crack. It was one floor down from my grandparents' room, and Dad always bore the loud noise though he was a man who appreciated quiet. He also suffered from migraines. Whenever I would peek into Dad's study, sometimes I found him holding his head as he read. The blasting TV sure didn't help him.

Because my parents never made a big deal out it, I barely noticed the challenges of having my grandparents live with us. Now as a parent, I can hardly imagine how my parents must have felt about all this. I mean, our lifestyle was definitely affected by having our grandparents living with us. For example, even our trash was affected. Now Mama was the sweetest thing, but every week, she scoured every trashcan in the house, then packaged, and prepared it for trash day. First, she collected all the trashcans into one spot. Emptying one trashcan into another, she would consolidate the trash into fewer bags all the while pulling out anything she spotted useful. She didn't want to waste anything. Then after checking the trash, she would take a piece of string or ribbon from her pocket and neatly tie each bag.

Mom always told us that if we wanted to throw something away, we should wait until my grandparents visited my aunt. If we weren't strategic in our trash disposal, what went in the trashcan, if salvageable, would always find its way out.

Though I grew up in a wealthy neighborhood, it was practices like these that gave me an awareness of the poverty my grandparents lived in earlier in their lives; it also taught me not to take the affluence my family had for granted. These were valuable lessons learned, but can you imagine how Mama's digging through our trash could have caused some frustration and tension in the house?

This was intergenerational dorm life—lots of noise, little privacy, and a whole lot of personalities.

ENCOURAGING INVOLVEMENT

Despite struggles, our family's intergenerational household was effective. Everyone helped out. As my grandparents neared their mid-nineties to early hundreds, outsiders often commented how wonderful it was to have such involved grandchildren. Here's the deal—our parents set the example. We just followed them.

In Asian culture, there is a high regard for the elderly. Older adults I've worked with and who come from different backgrounds have always been appreciative of that. This cultural practice has everything to do with example. Our parents cared for their parents. Our grandparents cared for their parents too. The good news is you don't have to be Asian to create a culture of respect for elders in your homes or community.

Truthfully, I'm pretty sure Mom and Dad didn't join forces and have my grandparents move in with us because it was convenient for them. Quite honestly, it made their life harder. Yet as they intentionally committed to serve, there were little people watching. Little people who watched the respect and honor given to the elders. Little people who watched compassion, sacrifice, and love offered to the old. When everyone in the house values grandparents or aging parents, intergenerational living is so much more effective, but it comes when parents teach by example.

Not only did my parents set an example for my sisters and me, they were also wise in the way they approached intergenerational living. If you already have an intergenerational household or are considering it, here are two important lessons I learned from parents.

First, if you are considering having aging parents move in, only decide to invite them if all parties agree. Before my sisters and I were born, Mom and Dad made the decision to invite my grandparents to live with them; most importantly, they made the decision together. Tracking back, when Mama and Yeye immigrated to the States, they first attempted to live on their own. Yet in a new country, with a new language, a house to maintain, and no car, my grandparents only survived a short stint of living independently. In my family's case, living with Mama and Yeye was not simply my dad inviting his parents to live with us; this was a joint decision, and one that only would have occurred with my mom's consent. Because the road of caregiving can be trial-filled, everyone (at least the people in charge) needs to be committed to caring for older family members.

Similarly, if you are considering living with aging parents, be sure to value your elders with the same love you offer to your children (if you're a parent). As one of my sisters noted, "Don't treat them like second-class citizens." As I look back, I notice that my parents considered Mama and Yeye as part of our immediate family. When looking for a larger home to accommodate our entire family (children and grandparents included), they purposely looked for good schools, but also a home that was close to public transportation, taking into account that my grandparents couldn't drive. They always saved Mama and Yeye a good-sized bedroom, and they even reserved the one bathroom on the top floor of our house for my grandparents. I should point out, there was only one bathroom on the top floor and my parents could have given it to my sisters and me. But my parents knew it would be most convenient for Mama and Yeye to have a bathroom on that floor, and without a beat, my sisters and I were instructed to use the bathroom three floors down. This act of respect was something that went unnoticed for me as a child, but now I think of that bathroom and it serves as a visual reminder of how we can value and honor the old in tangible ways. Without saying a word, my parents showed my sisters and me how to honor our elders.

The Best Living Arrangement

I used to think living with the older adult was the best way to care for them. Without a doubt, my family offered Mama and Yeye an exceptional quality of life; they lived a long and full life, and I believe caring for them in-house had a lot to do with it. But over the years as I've worked in the senior living environment, I observed families who, like mine, showered their older relative with love, yet their elder didn't live with them. This is what I've found: no living arrangement automatically guarantees the best quality of life for our older relatives.

Here's the thing. After serving elders for years inside and outside my home, I discovered a comforting truth: we don't have to live with elders to love them, but we *do* need to include them in our lives. An elder can live with family and feel just as lonely as they would in a senior care community. An elder can live in a senior community and feel just as loved as they would if they lived with family at home. When we include the older generation in our conversations, events, and lives, this is how they know we care. We include people in our lives to remind them that they matter.

"I wish people knew that you can't include them in everything, but there are many important activities that you can include them in. Birthday parties and

Christmas. If they are living in the facility, go to the facility and bring them home so they can enjoy the holiday with family. Because when you don't bring them in on the family, they feel left out."

MARY, 85

Look around: The most content older people can be found when they are surrounded by those they love. And it's not that they need to be part of everything; all they want is to be invited.

When someone receives an invitation, they hang it up in a visible place. It reminds them of an actual event, but it also serves as a reminder that someone is thinking about them. But that's not all. When someone receives an invitation, they talk about it. They tell others they're invited or going to this event. They think and plan their outfit. They figure out transportation. When we send an invitation to someone, whether it be a concert, a party, or a program, we make them feel special knowing they are a part of something. They feel valued.

If you desire to bless an older person, be sure to include and integrate them in your life. This is what they want. If your grandparents or aging parents live far away, this may look different. But these days, we can connect with people well even if they live across the country or overseas. The small gestures we make can communicate to a person that we care for them.

When it comes to a formal invitation, Grandma may not be able to come to every party or event. As health declines, this will become truer. But don't let that keep you from inviting her. In fact, consider how empowering it could be for

Grandma to decline your offer. Sure, it will make her feel sad for not being able to come, but it will leave her beaming knowing that you took time to invite her; you remembered her. Your invitation speaks volumes.

The best part about invitations, whether formal or not, is it gives our older friends something to look forward to. They can have fun bragging about it. "My daughter is going to take me out to lunch today," or "Next month, I'm flying to New York to watch my grandson graduate," or "My grandson loves football and he asked *me* to come to a game."

Have you been wondering how you can bless the old? Then, extend an invitation to your elder. Include them in your life. Let them be your guest of honor. And give them a reason to smile.

....

TAKE NOTES | *How to Include Older Adults in Our Lives*

Including an older person into our everyday life is one of the best ways to love and to speak life into that person. Here are some ideas to get your grandparents, aging parents, or friends involved in your family and the community around them:

1. EXTEND AN INVITATION

Invite them out for a meal or coffee.
Invite them to parties, sports events, or recitals.
Invite them to visit a new place.

Plan a vacation together.

Invite them to take a walk with you.

Go shopping together.

2. INCLUDE THEM IN CONVERSATION

Ask if they can hear you. Speak louder if needed.

Hold their hand or place your hand on their arm as a way to acknowledge them.

Explain terms, places, gadgets, technology, and programs to ensure older adults can engage in the conversation. Help them understand what you're talking about.

Ask "How are you?" or "What have you been doing lately?" or "What do you think?" to show you are interested in them and to engage in more conversation.

3. STAY CONNECTED

If moving them to a senior living facility is necessary, find a facility that makes it convenient for you to visit often.

Periodically connect through snail mail, text, email, or video chat to ask how they are doing.

Communicate and update them on life regularly through email, phone calls, or video chats.

Send them gifts so they know you are thinking about them.

On a regular basis, ask how you can help them.

Schedule periodic trips where your purpose is both to offer a helping hand and to spend time with them.

4. HOST CELEBRATIONS WITH THEM IN MIND

Incorporate food into the meal that they can and like to eat. (Sometimes this means softer food. Sometimes this means soups.)

Arrange transportation if needed so they can attend family or community events.

Check in with them periodically at an event to see how they are doing and if they need anything.

For children's birthday parties, make arrangements so they have a gift to give. This may involve helping them purchase and wrap a gift.

Plan a birthday celebration or an anniversary celebration with them, asking them for input on the details.

chapter 4

REAL-LIFE
ENCOUNTERS

During my senior year of college, the thing on my mind and my mom's was that I needed a job. Any job. As a freshman, like many others, I had been "undecided." Undecided with a genuine interest in seven different majors.

Art majors endured extreme sleep deprivation (which I could not handle), and though I liked to write, I never felt good at it. Sophomore year, I decided to major in Business Administration. During my senior year, with a degree almost in hand, I searched for all types of jobs, dreaming and wondering what I might become.

One fall afternoon, as I strolled across campus, I stopped by the Resident Life office to visit a friend who worked there. Pushing open the glass door, I found myself stepping right into an informal conversation between several staff members about an upcoming board meeting. Resident Life was looking for senior students to share their future aspirations with board members.

A few weeks later, I found myself eating a fancy meal at that same board meeting. Several students had already shared their ambitious and concrete plans. Then it was my turn. I bashfully stood up before the board members and smiled. "I'm thinking about working with kids . . ." then I threw in, "or working with seniors. I'm not really sure."

Though far from impressive, when the meeting adjourned, one of the board members approached me. "There's a huge need for good nursing home administrators," he told me. Bob Van Dyk owned a family-run senior living facility and had been working in the field for years. The father of a classmate, he graciously offered to meet to discuss possibilities. What? A possible job lead? Now that sounded exciting to me.

Before meeting Mr. Van Dyk, I'd always assumed that in order to work with the elderly, I'd have to become a nurse. The kind that changes bed pans. So while I was *thinking* about working with the elderly, I wasn't keen on that.

I imagine most college grads go for well-charted territory. Accounting, engineering, consulting, advertising, teaching. I, too, planned to walk that path. But that evening, Mr. Van Dyk piqued my interest and opened my eyes to the possibilities in the field of aging. After that meeting, he connected me to Erickson Living, a solid senior living company based in Maryland. Thanks to him, a few months later, I accepted my first real job out of college! I was grateful for a job. *Any* job. I had no idea, however, where this job would lead me.

A FUTURE IN THE AGING FIELD

The job referral came at the perfect time. That year, Erickson Living started the Operations Associate program, an initiative aimed at training young professionals to be future leaders in the aging field.

This program allowed a young person to become acquainted with various departments throughout the company in order to find their niche. Rotations offered me glimpses into several departments and showed me that with every skill set, there was a job to match it in the industry. I observed social workers as they guided and supported residents struggling with physical, mental, and emotional issues. I tagged along with volunteer management as they coordinated their next volunteer appreciation event. I shadowed security as they monitored the hallways, housekeepers as they cleaned toilets, and administrators as they handled complaints or prepared for inspection. I spent time in the fitness center (where I took my next job). I even spent time in the laundry room, where I learned one of the greatest tips of all time—how to fold fitted sheets.

In a short period of time, my understanding of the senior care industry grew tenfold. No longer did I think every place where older people lived was a nursing home. Instead, I learned different facilities offered different levels of care dependent on the individual's health needs. For example, Erickson Living retirement communities offered all three levels of care in one place: independent living, assisted living, and skilled nursing with short-term rehab.

When an older adult needs more than the typical amount

of care, people automatically think they need to live in a nursing home. But I learned what the other options are. In terms of housing, independent living offers housing for older people without any personal assistance (unless private care-givers are hired). Assisted living offers individuals help with a various level of activities of daily living, such as changing clothes, medication reminders, etc. Skilled nursing, which we commonly know as the nursing home, is where individuals go who have the most complex medical issues and need 24-hour medical care. I should note that nursing homes also offer short-term rehabilitation where people can receive in-house physical, occupational, or speech therapies to help them recover after a hospitalization or surgery.

As I absorbed all this information, I stowed it away knowing one day it might come in handy. Especially at home.

A WHOLE NEW WORLD

Have you ever traveled to a foreign country? Take one step off the plane and life looks, smells, sounds, and even tastes completely different. The chairs have a different feel to them, the bathrooms aren't quite what you're used to. People talk and even walk in a different manner. This is what happened to me. When I started my first job, I went from hanging out with the college crowd to seeing older people Monday through Friday. This was culture shock. I had entered a whole new world.

In no time, I realized how little I actually knew about older people. Come to think of it, my understanding of aging came from limited exposure to the elderly. My perceptions evolved out of my weekly 15-minute visits with Burt and Elsie during my college ministry experience and living with my grandparents. And while my exposure might have been more than what many other 21-year-olds experienced, it was four people in total that I had based my perceptions on. Four people out of millions.

A Closer Look

When I rotated through different departments in the Operations Associate program, I didn't have much direct interaction with residents. Yet two years later, I accepted a permanent placement in the Wellness Center at Erickson Living's Riderwood community in Silver Spring, Maryland. That is where I came face-to-face with hundreds of residents.

With each new Riderwood resident I met, the more I saw the diversity of personalities, experiences, challenges, and preferences of the older person. I could no longer label an older person as "old" and "slow." Every resident proved to be different.

> *"Well, if you haven't started walking,*
> *it's never too late to start.*
> *Do it whenever you can regularly."*
>
> **WALT, 98**

In the beginning, getting to know these elders was a bit daunting. Around me stood people with Parkinson's who shook with tremors, were bent over severely, and spoke abnormally slow. There were people with Alzheimer's who wandered up to me and were sometimes confused. Walkers, scooters, and even wheelchairs were all over the place.

Certain instances really scared me. Like when a man with an oxygen tank and a tube stretched across his nose walked in the doors of the fitness center. I remember freaking out. If I accidentally bumped his oxygen tank, would he stop breathing? If he started exercising, was it possible he might keel over and die?

He was fine. Thanks to the mentorships of many colleagues, supervisors, and leaders in the company, I quickly learned not to underestimate an older adult's capabilities. From residents, I started to learn a lot about the physical health of older adults too. In conversation, residents would bring up the health issues they were facing. And I became familiar with words like COPD, stents, pacemakers, sciatica, fibromyalgia, or macular degeneration. When I encountered a new term, I asked questions, I read articles, I learned. I gained a better picture of the health issues older adults face, and I gained a greater respect for what they're up against.

"Firsts"

In my role as a Wellness Coordinator, I trained and encouraged residents in their exercise routines. Every day, around a hundred residents came in and out the doors of the fitness center.

In meeting all these people, I experienced a number of "firsts." Like seeing excessively dry and flaky skin or observing someone's legs swelled almost to the point of bursting. I remember helping a lady whose hands were abnormally deformed. "Rheumatoid arthritis," a colleague told me.

On one particular day, I saw a couple strolling down the hallway hand in hand. *How sweet!* I thought. Much to my surprise, I discovered this husband held his wife's hand, *yes,* because he loved her, but also because she had Alzheimer's and was known to wander.

Despite some shocking firsts, work was actually quite fun. No one took their teeth out for me (that could have triggered a career change) or hit me with their cane. One resident, when I mentioned how nice her hair looked, did giggle and wink, as she shifted her wig to let me in on her secret.

One of the nice parts about working in a retirement community was that the residents often grew fond of the employees who served them. They especially loved talking with younger folks. At the time, I was 23, and residents were eager to hear about my hobbies, future dreams, and family. They would ask about my culture; some, of course, even wanted to know about potential soul mates. From this, unexpected friendships evolved.

Take Harold, for example. He didn't say much, but one day I shared with him how my boyfriend liked to fish. The next time he came in to exercise, he walked straight into the office and handed me a plastic container. "Give it to your boyfriend," he said, "and make sure you stick it in the fridge." Little did I know that I had been given a container of night crawlers to pass on to Kevin. It was a thoughtful gesture.

When I decided to apply for a Master's in Public Health (MPH) program, Dolores and I hit it off. She had an MPH from the University of Michigan and for decades worked in public health. With the field I aspired to, Dolores cheered me on with her gentle spirit; we always had something to chat about.

Then there was Stan, who because of a rare condition was bent over almost 90 degrees. The first time I saw him, I was nervous. But once he spoke, I discovered that Stan was one of the most delightful residents on campus. He would strut into the fitness center, and though his head was always face down, you could tell he was smiling. Everyone liked him.

> Older adults are not just "old." Older people can be intriguing, inspiring, exciting, and funny; they can be delightful, loving, and ultimately the most humble and kind of people.

Finally, if I needed a laugh, there was George. While he visited the fitness center regularly, he'd come in, walk thirty seconds on the treadmill, press the red stop button, and call it quits. Then he'd turn around and strike up a conversation with the nearest person around him.

> *"A sense of humor is a great thing to have when you're getting old. If you laugh at things it makes it much easier. And friends, close friends, friends that you can laugh with."*
>
> **JANICE, 86**

The more time we spend with others, the more we learn about them. With each new experience, I kept on learning. I learned how big band music switched a light in some residents and got their whole bodies and heads bopping. I learned how certain news channels irritated residents and got them growling. It was in that fitness center where I spent millions of minutes developing friendships with older folks, some of whom I still keep in touch with.

In hanging with the older crowd Monday through Friday, I discovered something amazing. Older adults are not just "old." Older people can be intriguing, inspiring, exciting, and funny; they can be delightful, loving, and ultimately the most humble and kind of people.

I NEVER KNEW

In my youth, I naturally thought about myself and didn't take the time to think about the life of an older person. When I started working with seniors, though, I uncovered struggles that many of the residents at my retirement community dealt with. Ones I never considered. For one, I never knew all the emotions a senior experiences when they have to move.

At Riderwood (and I'm sure at other senior living communities too), a number of residents moved into the retirement community not entirely by choice. Their family or spouse pushed for the move; a health issue often necessitated it too.

I met many residents reluctant to move in. These residents often headed to the fitness center first as they wanted to be around the most active and lively, not the hundreds of other "old" people around. Fitness center policy required new residents to meet with a Wellness Coordinator before they used equipment, so there I found myself in many conversations that often landed on the topic of unwanted transition. Time and time again, residents would tell me how hard it was for them to leave "home," a place where they started and raised their families, where they lived for decades.

Today when I hear an older person share about a move or a downsize, I sense the grief that comes with losing their home. Though moving out may provide a safer and more practical environment for their season in life, you hear seniors share how they miss the freedom, space, and the memories they leave behind. They miss the yard, their dinnerware, their kitchen equipment, the extra bathroom, the studio or garage; they even miss the smaller items they may have had to get rid of.

"Move to assisted living before you have to. It's easier for you and it's easier for everybody else. One thing that I don't like about this [assisted living] is a lack of privacy because people are coming in at all hours of the day and night. Sometimes they don't make the bed the way I think it ought to be."

WALT, 98

An elderly person's belongings become a touchy subject as they age. Have you ever tried talking to a senior about cleaning up their clutter or observed them in a downsize? They can't let go. But that's because our belongings are important to us. One older lady shared with me how her friends who moved to assisted living were angry with their adult children, to the point that they stopped talking to them. Without their permission, their children had thrown away many of their belongings. Sometimes in our hurry to clear out a space, we destroy some of the things that make our elder feel secure.

When it comes to the belongings of our grandparents and parents, remember to be cautious in the way you deal with their "stuff." Remember that their belongings are attached to memories. And as they lose their spouses or other loved ones and lose their good health, their belongings become the one tangible thing they can control and hold onto. Consider this before you discard anything that belongs to an elderly person.

In uncovering the struggle with transitions and the importance of an elder's belongings, I also came to see how important independence was to them. During the month that I rotated and shadowed the social work department, I sat in on resident assessments before they moved in. After two assessments, something stood out to me. Every resident showed an unusual determination to excel on the test, as if their life depended on it. If asked to count backwards from twenty, he or she did it as quickly as possible. When asked a question, the individual responded with rapid fire. If asked to walk a straight line, the person was cautious, yet swift in completing the task. No joke, this test was serious business to them.

It was odd at first to see the urgency behind each response or action. Then I realized the reason for the rush: the results of the assessment would affect the individual's placement in the community. This evaluation determined whether they could live on their own or with assistance. There was no room for physical or mental weakness. If the social worker deemed an individual appropriate for assisted living instead of independent living, that would be the greatest letdown. Understanding the struggles of an older adult is an important step in learning how to love them.

They Have Goals, Too

There's even more depth to an elder than simply their struggles. What I love about meeting older adults is that they all have a rich story and wealth of experience that can only occur with time. Take a look at the experience of some real-life people who are in their sixties and beyond:

Former/current jobs: foreign language teacher, attorney, special agent for the FBI, manager of a trucking company, secretary, air force, corporate trainer, builder, social worker, librarian, accountant, electrical engineer, sales manager, banker, nurse educator, research analyst, seamstress.

Sometimes we believe that because someone is old, they are done with life. But when you spend time with older people, you might be surprised to see they still have ambitions for the future. Look at the goals of some real-life people, again who are in their sixties and beyond:

Future goals: to have long life, to write a book, to have good relationships with husband and children and to see grandchildren do wonderful things, to please my Maker, to enjoy life, to live independently the rest of my life, to have good health, to travel and walk without a cane, to help those less fortunate, to learn more about genealogy, to expand computer skills.

....

In some ways, older people are just like us; they're simply older. Behind the label of "old," every older person has a depth to their life, past, present, and future. That, to me, is so cool.

IT WASN'T SMELLY. IT WAS DIFFERENT.

When I first toured an Erickson Living retirement community, I was 21 and impressed, not to mention surprised. This was a place for *old* people, yet it didn't feel (or smell) like anything I had ever seen before. The community was designed like a college campus, encouraging a healthy and active community; it was livelier than you'd expect, if you know what I mean. Remember how in my college years, I thought the only way to serve older adults was to be a nurse? Well, stepping into this type of retirement community changed everything. It gave me hope when I thought about the future of my grandparents.

It wasn't that I wanted Mama and Yeye to move into an Erickson Living retirement community; it was more that I now had a new template, a much better example of how to bless elders, but it was far more impressive than changing bedpans. See, I found an organization that really thought about the older adult's needs and intentionally, through design and details, tried to help them thrive. For example, Riderwood, where I worked, has weatherproof walkways allowing residents to walk to any place on campus without stepping a foot outdoors. Physicians, dentists, eye doctors, and podiatrists are on-site. There is a pharmacy, a fitness center, a pool, a bank (yes, the kind with lollipops), and even a mobile post office, which visits the campus regularly. Shuttles offer transportation around the community, but they also offer trips to the supermarket or even to the mall. Crafts studios, card rooms, movie nights, shows from famous Broadway singers or well-known musicians, and clubs of all kinds meet the interests of different older adults. The interesting thing is that clubs only are formed if residents are willing to run them. Thus, these clubs are simply a menu for elders; they give these residents work that motivates them. My favorite club was the Habitat for Humanity group, which was composed of a group of men who built shelves in the woodshop on campus and donated them to Habitat for Humanity.

In promotion of life-long learning, Riderwood still has partnerships with the community college, which offers over fifty classes per semester on the facility's campus, so that residents can take noncredit courses throughout the year. When I asked one of the residents how he was doing one day, reminiscent of the average college student, he said, "It was good until yesterday. I didn't get into the classes I wanted."

With classes like Whimsical Grammar or Golden Days of Radio, registration fills up quickly. I, for one, hope they still offer the class on First Ladies when I get old.

You wouldn't expect it, but the residents at these communities, who are anywhere from 62 to over 100, are not just sitting around. One of my 81-year-old friends said, "I thought I was going to sit in a rocking chair." Instead, she volunteers, has dinner dates with friends, and sells her own jewelry made out of church bulletins. She stays in touch with her kids and grandchildren. She regularly sees her sister. She keeps busy.

The truth is the residents of these communities are still aging. They still hit decline. But the best of these types of communities offer hope in this season. They provide us with an example of how we can engage, encourage, and help older adults thrive in whatever community they live in. We can't stop aging, but we can work hard to offer the best support and environment for it.

DETAILS MATTER:
MEALS AND MAILBOXES

In our own communities and activities, certain populations often are forgotten in the planning stages and, thus, forgotten in the details. As a result, some of the hippest and nicest places in town are closed off to certain populations. Consider the accessibility of community programs or resources and how at times it excludes those with physical disabilities. With not enough handicap parking or the lack of a ramp or elevator, certain groups of people are truly blocked off from community.

When I look at exceptional elder care models, I see a prime example of how our families, neighborhoods, churches, or other communities can become more welcoming environments for older adults. A simple way Erickson Living promotes a senior friendly community is by adding benches throughout the hallways and walking paths. These are the types of details we can think of adding in our own neighborhoods. Benches make a world of difference for an older adult. He or she may want to stay active, but may not be able to find a spot to rest in the middle of a walk. When we are aware of their needs, we start seeing how the details matter.

Recently, I had the honor of sitting down with John Erickson, the founder and innovator of Erickson Living. Fascinated by the community's design, I asked him to share some "details" that he intentionally built into the very first communities. "Two things that [I thought] would ruin a community are to deliver the mail and to let the meal program be optional because then people have incentive to eat Campbell soup, save $5, and have no social structure. The whole design of the campus is to create spaces that attract people."[1] In keeping with that, placing mailboxes at the community center forces residents to come out of their apartments.

> When I look at exceptional elder care models, I see a prime example of how our families, neighborhoods, churches, or other communities can become more welcoming environments for older adults.

A lady sees her friend in the hallway and says, "Well, I haven't seen you in a long time!" And then they catch up.

Creating spaces for older adults helps them to thrive. They can adopt new hobbies, try new things, and connect with others. They can contribute.

THE RESULT OF
REAL-LIFE ENCOUNTERS

Spend enough time with Chinese people, and you'll quickly realize that our lives are more than lo mein and eggrolls. When we have real-life encounters with older adults, the same holds true: we realize there's more to the person than their "old" bodies.

A decade has passed since I befriended many of those sweet older friends from my fitness center days. Interestingly enough, my mom moved into Riderwood a few years ago. As a result, I have had the honor of seeing some of my "old" friends again. To be honest, after ten years, the health of every one of them has declined. They move slower than before. Some, who were avid walkers, now sit in wheelchairs. Others tell me how their spouses, who I also knew, have since died. The signs of aging are obvious, but I remind myself not to focus on them.

The real-life encounters I've had with friends decades ahead of me have taught me an important lesson: older adults have more to them than the physical signs of aging or what the media portrays. Behind their wrinkled exteriors are people with interests, passions, insights, thoughts, experiences, and adventures. Most of all, they have a rich story within, waiting to be discovered.

....

TAKE NOTES | *It's Never Too Late for Love*

At the gym, I recently met a delightful 85-year-old Italian woman named Dora. While she's one of the older ones in her crew of girlfriends, she proves to be one of the liveliest. But this is not the only way she has broken the typical stereotype of older people. Dora is a classic example of how it's never too late for adventure, fun, or even love.

About seven years ago, Dora attended a support group for widows and widowers. She was in charge of refreshments. One day, a male attendee walked over to the refreshment table and poured a glass of wine. The only problem was he refused to give a dollar donation, even after Dora prodded him to do so.

Disgusted, she cried, "Who is that old man?"

"Dora, be nice to him. He just lost his wife," her friend reminded her.

To which Dora responded, "I don't care. I lost my husband too."

A month later, that same man called Dora and asked her out to dinner. "Are you crazy? I have been alone for twenty-eight years. I never went out with anybody," she told him. But because her friends were out of town that weekend, she obliged. Dinner came and went and Dora was still not impressed.

Two weeks later the man who refused to give a dollar for donation called again, but this time he invited Dora out to dance. "I *love* to dance," Dora told me midway in her story.

After a year of dancing together, Dora and this man tied the knot and now have enjoyed the last six years together.

chapter 5

AN UNTAPPED RESOURCE

"I killed Herman!" I heard Barb tell her friend. And then she laughed.

Barb was in her eighties and came to work out with her husband quite regularly. I was 23 and still working in the Riderwood fitness center. Thus far, I'd overheard many conversations as people worked out, but never one quite like this.

Praise God, I found out "Herman" was not a person or even an animal. It was the name for Barb's sourdough starter. Starters, I learned from Barb, are like half-started recipes used to bake delicious breads or cakes. After receiving a starter, you grow and feed it by adding more ingredients. If you grow it well, your starter can multiply; this allows you to share "Herman" with others. If you neglect "Herman," the yeast may become inactive . . . and that's when the "killing" occurs.

The next time Barb visited the fitness center, she brought

me a Herman of my own. It came with five pages of instructions. "The day you receive a starter, place it in a large Tupperware bowl with a lid," it read, with a final reminder on page five: "Don't forget to stir it every other day." Barb gave me her phone number in case I had questions.

When it came time to bake something, the sourdough coffee cake using Barb's starter and instructions was amazingly delicious. Surprisingly tasty coming from a newbie in the kitchen like myself. Without Barb's direction, I'm sure I would have killed "Herman." But she was there to guide me along.

....

I've always enjoyed learning from the older crowd, specifically when it came to the kitchen. Marion gave me her pumpkin bread recipe. Judy typed out the instructions for a simple banana bread that didn't require a fancy mixer. Clara handwrote the six steps to making her Graham Cracker Plus dessert. Walt made copies of his 1972 bread recipe. And Churalene shared her corn pudding recipe, one she guaranteed was easy and that was sure to please.

Particularly in my post-college years, I benefited from the guidance of generous "cooking instructors" both in and out of the workplace. You see, I'm not naturally skilled in the kitchen arena, so by no means did I transform into an expert chef. But the tips from more seasoned "kitcheners" were priceless; they allowed for less failure. I didn't need to sift through hundreds of recipe books. I didn't have to waste pounds of flour. Instead, these older friends gave me an advantage. They shared favorite recipes from worn-out personal cookbooks, tweaked and taste-tested for decades by children, grandchildren, neighbors, and friends. This, my friends, is only one example of how the older generation is an untapped resource.

IN SEARCH OF SOLUTIONS—
GOOGLE VS. GRANDMA

When conflict arises in the kitchen, at school, work, in our homes, or even in our country, where do we go *first* for advice? Do we make a beeline to the oldest person in the room? Or jump in our cars and search out the nearest senior center? Far from it. When someone ages, we often decide they no longer have the ability or "right mind" to make good choices or to give sound and wise counsel. For advice, we usually go elsewhere. Google easily beats out Grandma.

I am one of those gals who can waste an entire night on the internet. I've searched homes for sale when I'm not in the market to buy one and tips on how to manage my frizzy hair. I can find the closest and cheapest parking for a family outing, and I can research 100,000 articles on the danger of tick bites. I "Yelp" any time Kevin and I snag a date night. I use Pinterest when a kid's birthday rolls around, and I watch YouTube when we need to fix a broken appliance. And then when I'm depressed, feeling anxious, or just worn down from motherhood, I do what everyone else does: I type words in the search bar. And hope to find an answer. Any answer.

"Have interests other than just your work,
because lots of people get so wrapped up
in their work."

WILLIAM, 85

It's amusing how in our search for solutions, we turn to the "cloud" and click on unreliable and sketchy links. I do it because it's easy. Ironically, with today's technology, just as easily we have access to "hotlines" with decades of practical experience. Within walking distance, we can meet people full of nearly limitless wisdom.

BETTER THAN A STUDY GUIDE

A few years after graduating, I decided to pursue my master's degree but hit an annoying roadblock. The GREs. The problem with standardized tests is I rarely do well on them. I don't have a photographic memory, and my vocabulary never includes words like obsequious, ameliorate, or capricious.

That's why when I took the GREs the first time, I scored low—low enough that after I applied to the Master's in Public Health program at the University of Maryland, I was rejected. Determined, I signed up for the GREs a few months later. For my first round, I'd studied in the office when the fitness center was in a lull. The second time, however, I tried a different approach: I left the solitude of the office and enlisted the help of residents.

While residents walked on the treadmill, I stood beside

them. When they biked, I sat on the recumbent bike to keep them company. And as they exercised, I reviewed vocabulary words. *What does audacious mean?* I would ask. And Bob would give me his own definition. *How would you use that in a sentence?* And Dolores would think of a way to use the term. After a day of this new method, I found studying with the residents far more interesting than memorizing the GRE study guide. The definitions and examples these folks created were also far easier for me to remember.

So, when I took the GREs the second time around, what do you think happened? I actually recognized and knew the answers to many questions. As a result, I did it! I scored higher marks on the verbal section. The following semester, I was offered admission into the University of Maryland, College Park's Master's in Public Health program.

THE QUALIFICATION OF AN EXPERT

Do anything for a decade, and you will be experienced in your craft. Wash five loads of laundry a day for ten years, and you will have figured out the fastest way to clean clothes. Chop trees for twenty years, and you'll have discovered the most efficient way to chop wood. Fish for thirty years, and you will have perfected the technique to lure fish. Teach for forty years, and you'll have nailed down the skill of classroom management.

The elders in our midst may no longer look that polished. But under their belt, they have sixty, seventy, or even eighty-plus years of expertise. Newsflash: *every* older adult excels at something. Thus the experience older adults have is something to be respected.

Imagine if, side by side, we laid the résumé of our elders next to ours:

OLDER ADULTS	MILLENNIALS
40 years working in the corporate world	15 years working in the corporate world
50 years fixing cars	15 years fixing cars
60 years of marriage	10 years of marriage
60 years of money management	3 years of money management
80 years of life	35 years of life

It's no question then that older adults have more experience than we do. Year after year, they gain more expertise —in living life, but also in a skill or trade. Their expertise may be career-related, hobby-related, relationship-related, quirky-tricks-related. Every year they gain something.

Similarly, we do too. So next time you may dread your next birthday, don't be filled with gloom, rather be filled with gratitude because with more years, each of us is guaranteed to be good at something. I'd say that's something to look forward to.

In the last few years, I've gained a genuine appreciation

for the discoveries that come with age. The discoveries that make life better. And more fun. Sometimes, I may miss my teen and twenty-something days, but . . . I really don't. Because with each year, I've made some major discoveries. I used the childcare at the gym and discovered the beauty of it. I learned about password management and have experienced the freedom of it. I've finally learned how to make meals without having a nervous breakdown. Just this year, I found a new brand of running shoe that feels more comfortable than ever. And get this. I've now honed my technique for thrift shopping. I've also figured out the perfect time for our family to go camping while also avoiding the mosquitos and the crowds. Score!

Contrary to what society tells us, we get better with time. We learn new strategies, processes, coping mechanisms, and insights. Sometimes, we even learn how to look better. Thus, we (even those of us who refuse to reveal our age) actually have a lot to celebrate. We have a lot to be proud of. Instead of a source of embarrassment, our age ought to be a badge of honor.

What's Your Opinion?

If we approached older adults whenever we were in search of sound advice, it would send a strong message of respect to our white-haired citizens. After thirty-five years of being around the old, I've learned to give more weight to the advice of those older than myself. An older adult's wisdom—and specifically their impressive résumé—gives me reason to listen.

"Wrinkles = wisdom"

SARAH, 71

While hanging out with girlfriends my age is life-giving to me, I've also come to see the advantage of having older friends, whether they are ten or fifty years ahead. There is a stark difference between asking a peer and someone older for advice. Recently, I'd been wrestling over whether to quit my job. I loved working, but at home, the tasks of feeding, clothing, and tracking three fast-moving kids day in and day out was tiring. No joke. Everyday responsibilities (like dishes and showering) were falling to the wayside.

It was a tough debate. One week I was determined to keep working. Another week, my body was pushed past exhaustion and I was sure I needed to let go. For about two years, I asked others for advice in search for a solution. After some time, I began noticing a difference.

When I talked to peers, most of them suggested I keep my job. *How can you find a job with such flexibility? It's a great outlet for you. You need a break from the kids.* That's exactly what I was thinking.

But when I asked older people, particularly those with grown children, almost every one shared that it was okay to ease off my career for this season. They had been through that same season and knew what I was up against.

Reaching a resolution was complicated, but in the end, I resigned from my job. Why? Because I realized my friends—who were looking out for my best interest—had not "been there, done that." Their advice, though loving, was shortsighted. But my older acquaintances had a long-term perspective; they knew the stresses of motherhood and the value of slowing down for the sake of family. One lady, now 86, even said that if she could go back in time, she wouldn't have worked so much.

Now don't get me wrong. And don't go quitting your job so soon either. In consulting someone older, we are not bound to take their advice, but we gain deep insight that may make us think twice.

Essentially, one word sums this up: wisdom. In the dictionary, wisdom is defined as "the quality of having experience, knowledge, and good judgment."[1] All too often we don't know how valuable wisdom truly is. We assume it's one positive quality, when in reality, it's a steal: three qualities in one. And really, I believe it's even better than that. The Bible says, "Does not long life bring understanding?" (Job 12:12b). When someone ages, their time on earth gifts them with far more perspectives than those who are younger possess. Elders are blessed with a deeper understanding of situations. When we ask our elders for insight, they won't gloss over our struggles and offer an opinion; instead, they can grasp our situations and offer us wisdom.

> My older acquaintances had a long-term perspective; they knew the stresses of motherhood and the value of slowing down for the sake of family.

THIS IS HOW I KNOW WHAT LOVE IS

Sometimes we glean from the older generation not from their words, but from their example. I prefer this because books and blah-blah-blah lectures slip and slide permanently through my memory most of the time. When it came to lessons from my elders, the most powerful ones, the ones I remember most, had to do with Mama. She never lectured me; she showed me.

In fact, Mama is the one who taught me about love. When it came to my grandparents' marriage, their relationship was far from perfect; it wasn't even romantic. Yeye directed and decided everything, from finances to involvement in events. Mama—like the "typical Asian woman"—was meek, gentle, compromising, almost too forgiving, and she always looked out for the needs of others. This included her husband.

About ten years ago, a few days into my marriage, Yeye suffered a stroke. He wouldn't survive in a split-level home, and so it became necessary to move him to an assisted living home after his rehab at a nursing home. Yet when it came to Mama, she really didn't need to move; she was perfectly healthy. Thus, as Yeye's rehab stay neared its end, our family urged Mama to consider staying at home, to not move to the assisted living with Yeye. Yeye had a bad temper, and because Mama often was the scapegoat, we were hopeful she would use this opportunity to separate; we wanted to protect her. When we talked to Mama, however, I vividly remember hearing her—with no hesitation—genuinely declare that until her husband died, she would stay with him. And so, when Yeye moved to the assisted living, she did too. She voluntarily subjected herself to a new home and a place not as comfortable or lively as what she was entitled to. But for one year, the year before Yeye passed, she stuck with it. She stayed in assisted living though she was far from needing assistance. She was keeping her vow. She was sticking to her commitment.

One year later, the day before Yeye died, I saw Mama live out love again. On a fall day after work, after receiving a report that Yeye was unusually weak, I drove to visit him. As I pulled my car into the driveway of the assisted living home and walked in quietly to the corner of the house, I came upon a scene, one of love in action.

Steps away, through the door frame, I caught a glimpse of Mama. Hunched over, at under five feet, she was standing at the side of Yeye's bed. With her 97-year-old frame, Mama held out her wobbly hand. She was already panting as she expended all her might to pull Yeye up. Yeye, I had been told, could no longer stand on his own. From a distance, I watched Mama grab a foam cup, positioning it in front of her husband's mouth. Though Yeye was without words, it appeared Mama knew what he needed. Yeye proceeded to vomit. A strong and strong-willed man, I'd never seen Yeye fatigued and fragile like that. I'd also never seen such an old lady labor so hard, so determined to help.

Nothing prepared me for what she showed me next. Seconds later as Yeye sweated to scoot to the edge of his bed, Mama propped her forehead up against his, and together the two toiled with many small movements to remove his pants. Next with her right hand, Mama reached for another foam cup. This time, she held it lower. Dark yellow pee dripped into the cup.

Initially, I felt disgust. That night as I drove home and I

processed what I had witnessed, I began to understand. Mama was determined to give her husband dignity. That day, there were no hearts flying, no romantic songs or fluttering feelings, but I witnessed love, the truest form of it. With her wrinkled, weak, and hunched-over body, Mama showed me what it might look like to love your spouse to the very end. That was better than any book could have taught me.

....

Are you mulling over a decision right now? Are you struggling to handle the responsibilities of life? Do you just need help to change a car light bulb? When a predicament comes your way, I want to plug a new type of search engine: consult an older friend for their perspective. Ask how they dealt with the same experience. Ask for an in-person tutorial on how it can be done.

As you listen, learn, and watch, take notes and please share! And remember that in our midst is a rich and untapped resource. The older crew is a decked out library of resources, one we need to utilize. As we reach out, and tap into what they have to give, it can bless us. And no doubt, it will honor them.

....

TAKE NOTES | *When You Ask Them, You Honor Them*

Asking an older adult about their life, thoughts, or insights is one way to honor them. It's also a great way to gain practical help. Here are some sample questions to help you learn from an older friend. Beware, it may also draw out an amusing story or fact along the way:

> What did you learn from being in the war?
>
> What's a tip you have for keeping the kitchen clean?
>
> How did you woo your wife? What was the best gift you gave her?
>
> What's your go-to recipe?
>
> How can you get little children to keep their shoes on and get in the car?
>
> How did you deal with stress earlier in life?

....

chapter 6

STEP UP

Do not call my three-year-old a baby. Just one word can transform my cute, easy-going, charming boy into a firecracker. With fangs. With no reserve, he *will* scream at you: "I am NOT a baby! I am a BIG boy!" And then you'll know that you clearly made the wrong word choice.

Sam is like most children; he does not respond well to being called little. Isn't it amazing that even young children want to be addressed with respect? If we choose to disregard their little selves, boy, will they let us know.

It's been said caring for old people is like caring for babies. Yet when I hear people call Grandma a baby, it rubs me the wrong way. I understand how vulnerable older adults are. I see striking similarities between infant and elder care. But this is what I have a problem with: If we call them babies, then why don't we treat them like babies? Because, babies get treated pretty darn well. But older people? That's a different story.

Having cared for the young and the old simultaneously,

I've noticed that older adults get the short end of the stick. It may be odd to evaluate baby care in a book about the elderly, but hang with me because I think we can learn something from this all. Assessing the ways our society values babies will not only reveal how senior care has been lacking in comparison; it can help us pinpoint how we can step up our game and offer better treatment to our elders. Sometimes we just need a guide and practical ways we can love the older folks in our lives. And that is exactly what this chapter is meant to do.

WHAT'S ALL THE EXCITEMENT ABOUT?

While I'm not an expert in much, I do know something about babies. Within four and a half years, I've been pregnant, given birth, and then cared for three milk-thirsty, diaper-filling babies. I'm fluent in baby whines and cries. I've gushed over chubby cheeks and thighs. I've wrestled to brush baby teeth, and I've dealt with babies' quirky sleeping and personalities. In short, I have lost sleep, weight, and sanity, all for the sake of beloved babies.

When a baby is on the way, excitement is in the air. The news breaks and people squeal and scream. They jump up and down and get giddy. They use exclamation points! They absolutely cannot contain themselves.

I was about two years into a new job when I had to deliver the news to my boss. I was pregnant. That day, I swiveled side to side in my chair as I sat in a weekly one-on-one with her. I knew I had to tell her, but no good moment came around.

With resolve, I blurted midway in the meeting, "I'm going to have a baby," and that's when my boss flipped. She jumped out of her chair and clapped uncontrollably. "This is the best news ever, Isabel!" she exclaimed.

From then on, the excitement did not end. A few days later, at our all-staff meeting, my boss, still bubbling, announced to everyone "we" (as in our department) were going to have a baby. Everyone cheered. Coworkers stopped me in the bathroom to share their personal birth stories; they glowed with delight at my growing belly. Everywhere I went, my unnamed baby received preferential treatment.

A month away from my due date, I'd toyed with the idea of painting the nursery, yet decided it'd be too much. Then, a friend offered to paint the room for us on her week off. Really? In a day, the room that had not been painted since we moved in finally got a fresh coat of sky blue. The crib was constructed. Baby décor was hung. Those weeks before baby came, we were completely focused on preparing a welcoming environment for baby.

When it comes to our older family members, they need people to get jazzed over them too. Whether it's singing "Happy Birthday" in unison, cheering them on in their physical therapy, or planning a sweet anniversary celebration, we can use our energy and excitement to shower love on the elder. It will feel good when they see someone goes all-out for them.

Think. Is it possible your grandparent or other aging adult in your life needs some true "baby-ing"? If you're looking for ways you can step up in enthusiasm for the older person you love, here are some ideas:

1. Cheerfully greet them every time you call or visit.

2. Take considerable time and thought to buy them a gift they would treasure.

3. Consider how you can help them create a better living space. Maybe their room doesn't need a coat of paint, but they could use darker shades to sleep better. Maybe you could print their favorite family pictures to make their room a more comfortable environment. Maybe they need a higher or more firm chair.

4. Plan a celebration with all the bells and whistles for them. Talk to them about who they want to be there and find ways to work in loving details such as their favorite food or music. Tell them you want to coordinate it for them.

NEW EXPERIENCES
AND REAL-LIFE INTERACTION

When I was pregnant with my third, my two other children, four and one at the time, had no compassion on my nausea and fatigue. On a regular basis, I stuck in a DVD and collapsed on the couch. I know watching TV all day is not ideal, especially for young children, but I was desperate. And so, Dora the Explorer? She became my back-up babysitter.

On one occasion, my daughter, Maddie, after watching at least two hours of this popular animated kids' show, walked over to the DVD player, shut it off, and scolded me, "Too much TV is not good for me, Mom."

No, sitting in front of the television all day long is not a healthy way of life. Those of us who are parents (and even those who aren't) know this. As a result, parents make it their goal to engage their kids' minds. For the sake of children, we have ridden park trains, hiked local nature centers, and trekked to the zoo even on hot days. We've researched art and music classes, looked into sports teams, and "road–tripped" to at least one amusement park. And finally on a quiet evening, even when our energy is low, we've read one more book aloud to the kids before bed. We do this all because we don't want our kids glued to a screen all day. We want to expose them to new things; we want their minds engaged.

Yet in the 15,600 nursing homes across the United States, blaring televisions are running all day long.[1] I give credit to activities departments that pack out calendars full of games, crafts, sing-a-longs, discussions, and events to engage a resident's mind. But I often wonder, how much healthier nursing home residents would be if they also had meaningful interaction through one-on-one conversations with familiar faces.

"I try to bless my grandpa by speaking in Chinese, even though both my grandpa and I know how poor my Chinese is. I think he gives me brownie points for effort."

JOSEPH, 31

I'd venture to guess that most seniors would be completely satisfied with regular calls or visits. But as grandchildren and young adults, we can do better than bingo; we can step up our game.

Brad Ryan, an adventurous and nature-loving guy, has done exactly that. In 2015, when Brad was visiting his 85-year-old grandma, he shared with her some of his outdoor adventures, only to find that his grandma, called "Grandma Joy," had never seen the oceans or the mountains. That conversation broke his heart, but it also convicted Ryan. It led him to invite his grandma to hike the Smoky Mountains with him. Four years later, Ryan and Grandma Joy, who is now 89, have trekked across the country to some of the most beautiful places around. They have graced twenty-nine national parks together including the Grand Canyon, Acadia National Park, and Great Sand Dunes to name a few.[2] That's awesome. And unbelievable.

I think we'd all yearn to be old if society gave all older people this type of special treatment. Grandma Joy is living a life that other older adults probably could never imagine. In her late eighties, she has stepped foot into some of the most awe-inspiring natural landmarks because of her grandson. More importantly, however, she has been blessed with millions of minutes to spend *with* her grandson. That is what I call meaningful interaction.

If you desire to shower your grandparent or aging parent with love, then engage them. As an older adult's social circles shrink and physical health weakens, they may feel cabin fever at times. When you help them "get out" and expose them to new things, you bring fresh air to the older adult's soul. Here are some suggestions on how to engage an older adult and provide them with more meaningful activities or conversation:

1. Find out what they like or don't like. To find new ways to engage your older friend, you need to spend time with the older person so you can discover "loves," "hates," wishes, and all. This provides a starting point for all sorts of fun activities and ways to engage that both of you will likely enjoy.

2. Create a bucket list. After learning more about your elder, brainstorm a bucket list of ideas on how to bring your loved one joy. Consider this a list of "to-dos" with your elder. Bring Grandpa on a fishing trip. Show him pictures of your latest catch. Bring Grandma to eat her favorite cuisine. Buy the cuisine at the store and bring it to her. Or buy the ingredients and cook it together.

3. Let them teach. If Grandma used to knit and crochet, ask her to teach you. If she shows no interest, learn on your own and show her your progress. She may add her two-cents. If you're working a yard project, ask Grandpa how he'd go about the project.

PUT GENEROSITY IN YOUR BUDGET

I've heard people say our wallet reflects our priorities. When it comes to our wallet, people shell out the big bucks for babies. They pay the extra dollar for the best daycare, the most engaging classes, and they will save up to buy the perfect gifts too.

When it comes to our elders, how much money do we spend on them? Traditionally in Asian culture, children set aside money and send it to their parents as a token of gratitude and respect. While we aren't obligated to pay for our parents' needs (at least in Western culture), does our wallet show we consider them a priority? Even more, are we willing to use our money to bless and support them?

I don't care if it was a random snack purchased with loose change, if someone bought me a gift every month, it would cheer me up. No matter what the dollar amount, when we spend money on someone, we send a message of love (especially to those whose "love language" is receiving gifts).[3] Here are simple ways we can use our wallets to bless:

Set aside money to pay for senior care expenses.
Buy the older adult a meaningful gift on birthdays and
    holidays.
Bring them flowers, a milkshake, or an apple pie when
    you visit.
Offer to treat them to a special meal or outing.

STOP HELPING THEM

While I am suggesting we treat older people with the same tender loving compassion that we offer babies, we have to remember that they are still adults who deserve a level of respect unlike no other generation.

Because they deserve respect, we need to be all the more

cautious in the way we treat our older friends and recognize some of the ways we unintentionally harm their well-being. In her book, *Cruising through Caregiving,* Jennifer FitzPatrick shares that sometimes we treat an aging parent like a child because it makes things easier or more efficient for us. "The caregiver thinks, *It takes my older loved one a long time to walk to the mailbox, so I'll just go ahead and mail her letters for her.*"[4]

FitzPatrick says that while this thinking can be rational, efficient, and even considerate, in the long run, it is a grave mistake and can make life harder for both us as caregivers and our aging loved one.[5] If we do too much for them, we may quicken their decline. Our helping can be harmful at times. Thus, *how* we help Grandma, Grandpa, Mom, and Dad requires wisdom.

If we truly want to position our grandparents or aging parents to thrive in old age, then our goal should be to preserve their independence as long as possible. When we start doing things for our loved ones simply because it is more efficient, we rob the older adult of their independence prematurely; we prevent them from exercising their physical and mental abilities. As the phrase goes, "use it or lose it."

Thus, even if it takes longer for Grandma or Mom to cook or it requires more time for them to complete a task, let them be. Let the older adult address a letter, wash their laundry, or even go to the bathroom on his or her own. Don't complete the task for them if at all possible, don't wheel them over when they can walk. Do show up and resolve to support them if needed. You want to provide support that allows them to do things themselves for as long as possible.

"I wish people knew that older people still in many
ways can take care of their own business.

I wish people knew that older people can still go to
the bank and deposit their checks
and cash their checks."

MARY, 85

THE DIGNITY OF RISK

When we try to preserve an elder's independence, we are doing them a great service. But what happens when grandparents or older parents start getting wobbly or shaky? Do we
put them at safety risk for the sake of independence? Early
in my career, I took a course at the University of Maryland,
Baltimore County, Erickson School of Aging. The course was
taught by Loren Shook, the CEO of Silverado Senior Living. In this course, Shook taught a concept first introduced by
Robert Perske called "the dignity of risk" that revolutionized
my perspective of quality senior care. It's something every person needs to know.[6]

The dignity of risk is all about treating people like humans
and giving them maximum independence. If you've ever cared
for someone whose health is declining, you might have seen
them do something unsafe or harmful to their health. Maybe
they wobbled as they walked, but decided not to use their
walker. Or maybe they needed exercise but refused. On the
sidelines, we may nag and say things like, "You *need* to use

your walker, Mom! You're going to fall!" Five minutes later, we repeat the same frustration, "Don't forget to use your walker, Mom!" When we direct their actions, we can dampen conversation. Even worse, we damage our relationship with the older adult. When someone feels like you're running their life, they will feel like you are ruining it too. What we need to recognize is how important it is to preserve our elder's dignity. Sometimes we prioritize safety over dignity and unintentionally do our elders harm.

At the heart of the dignity of risk is the idea that every human being should be able to make his or her own decisions and have the freedom to fail. Consider your own life and the choices you make. You may eat potato chips even though you know they're bad for you. You stay out in the sun longer, though you know you could get sunburn. You may walk on loose rocks across a creek, even though you possibly might fall. You take risks, and as humans, our ability to make our own choices preserves our dignity.

> Sometimes we prioritize safety over dignity and unintentionally do our elders harm.

As someone ages, if they are stripped from making their own decisions, this can lead to anger, resentment, and eventually apathy regarding one's own self. Because no longer does the older individual need to make decisions; others are making those decisions for them. Could this explain why in today's society so many older adults remain dull and unengaged?

Too easily, we get caught up in a wave of telling an older adult what to do. We can even make decisions for them without their consent. "Eat this. It's good for you." "You have to do this, Mom." The dignity of risk means that although we may not agree with their decisions at the time, we allow a person the freedom to make his or her own choices. Of course, there are times when allowing someone to put themselves at risk can be dangerous, or considered neglect, abuse, or just plain unethical. What we have to remember is that no black-and-white answer exists.

Consider these dilemmas: If an older adult falls or has some memory issues, do we tie them in a chair so it never happens again? Or if Grandpa has weak legs, yet refuses to use a cane, do we lock him inside the home? Most of the time balancing safety and dignity is a hard decision to make. Case by case, use your best judgment.

In the last thirteen years of Mama's life, she lived with my oldest sister, Jo, and her growing family. Naturally, there were many times when Jo and her family needed to leave the house either for activities or to run errands. When they had to leave, Mama, in her late nineties and early hundreds, often wanted to stay home. When Jo and her family were gone for short periods of time, though we worried about Mama's safety, we didn't force her to tag along. Mama knew the risk involved in staying home alone, so we gave her the option to choose. After all, it's not easy for a 100-year-old to tag along with a young family. Most of the time then, Mama chose to rest in her chair, with a phone in hand, as she waited until my sister came home. At times, we felt uneasy, and those of us who were available would check in on her by phone. But in offering Mama options—even though at times it presented a risk—I believe Mama felt more dignified because of it.

Balancing safety versus dignity is no easy task. The key is to be as hyper vigilant in preserving dignity as we are in providing safety. Sometimes in giving an older person freedom to fail, it may leave us feeling uneasy. But when we offer dignity to the older person, we value them respectfully as every human being deserves.

In the world of child development, offering babies tender loving care is crucial for early brain development. The nature of a baby's caretakers significantly impacts their future well-being. With nurturing and responsive caregivers, babies are more secure and confident as they explore the world. They also develop a better ability to manage stress.[7] Mental Health America states that having "unconditional love from family" and "encouraging teachers and supportive caretakers" are essential building blocks for good mental health in a child.[8] The benefits are clear.

It seems obvious then to say that when we shower our grandparents and older parents with a supreme level of love and attention, we can profoundly improve their well-being. We promote better physical and mental health. We can promote a more positive outlook on life. We encourage more stimulating conversation. We give them something new to talk about. We give them opportunities to learn and grow. We remind them they are not stagnant and open their eyes to experiences they would have not experienced otherwise.

Even when the rest of the world neglects our older generation, we can blast blessing into their lives. Not by gushing and gloating and giving them baby showers, but by giving them the same level of VIP treatment that we offer to our cute babies. So, let's use our creativity to inject some fun into Grandma's, Grandpa's, Mom's, or Dad's life. Let's step up our game in the way we care for our old. Let's refresh, redeem, and bring life to the older generation. Let's show them just how valuable they are.

....

TAKE NOTES | *Six Simple Ways to Offer Dignity to the Older Adult*

1. REMEMBER SENIORS HAVE MORE EXPERIENCE THAN YOU.

They may not be more intelligent or socially savvy than you, but based on their years, they do have more life experience than you. Respect them for it.

2. DON'T UNDERESTIMATE WHAT THEY'RE CAPABLE OF.

Just because your parent or grandparent is over 65 does not mean they can't do things on their own. Just because they're considered "senior" does not mean they shouldn't run, shovel, do yard work, etc. Unless the doctor rules out certain activities, or it is obviously dangerous, let them do what they want. Give them the freedom to fail at things.

3. DON'T DO EVERYTHING FOR THEM.

Many older adults are not weak simply from aging. They're weak because other people are doing things for them; they're not using their muscles or their mental abilities. They're not doing what they're fully capable of. The more an older adult does on their own, the longer they'll be independent as they age. The healthier they will be. When the time comes and they lose the ability to perform certain tasks, reality will show proof that it's no longer safe. This can lead naturally into a discussion on getting more help. In the meantime, let them get their own plate, collect the trash, and cook if they're able to. Sometimes they may mess up. But don't take control of tasks prematurely and enable inactivity.

4. ASK FOR THEIR INPUT.

Sometimes we won't be able to accommodate everything our older loved one wants, but in asking for their thoughts, we show we genuinely care and are looking out for their best interest. We communicate we are on their team. When we ask them, we honor them. And in asking, we develop trust, which is pivotal as elders get older and tough decisions regarding care or housing may need to be made.

5. ACKNOWLEDGE THEIR PRESENCE.

Especially as older adults become weaker or uncommunicative, families and even professionals often forget to acknowledge them. Whatever state an older adult is in, greet them. If they are nonverbal or unresponsive, place your hand gently on them so they know you are there. It's been said the last of the senses to be lost is often the sense of hearing. Instead of talking about a person, talk directly to them; include them in the conversation. You may need to patiently wait, but at least offer your loved one time to respond. Response may come through slow or nonverbal cues.

6. IF A PERSON HAS DEMENTIA OR IS LESS ABLE TO HELP, ALLOW THEM TO CONTRIBUTE WITH SMALLER TASKS.

Even with cognitive issues, older adults can help fold towels, fill the napkin holder, or peel string beans. You may have to "check their work," but when you make an effort to involve them, you give them a gift. The authors of *Keeping Love Alive as Memories Fade* say it best, "Whenever possible, do *with* rather than *for*." [9]

chapter 7

WHEN YOU'VE GOT A "LEMON"

Yeye was a tough cookie. Tough enough that, though he favored me, his behavior still rubbed me the wrong way and caused me to contemplate moving out a number of times. He was stubborn; he was also strong-willed. When he had a stroke, he refused to go to the hospital. When Dad finally got him to the hospital, he refused to go to rehab. When he finally obliged to go to rehab, we started getting phone calls. "Mr. To is going to the bathroom and getting up himself after we told him *many* times not to. It's *very* dangerous, and he could fall. You need to tell him not to go on his own," the staff would say. As if he would listen.

Yeye was defiant and demanding. He also tended to dramatize things. Take the night I brought him to the emergency room because of a severe nosebleed. Boy, did he give the ER doc a run for his money. Yeye wailed and flailed as the young doctor made several attempts to insert a plug into his nose. After several huffs of frustration, the doctor darted a look at me and, desperate, he yelled, "You have got to get him under control!"

....

There are nice old people and then there are difficult ones. In the back of your mind there may be a person who doesn't quite fit the rosy picture of the old I've painted thus far. The person you know reams people out. They disapprove. They nit-pick. They put up a fight for anything.

Dealing with people like this can really dampen your day. And because they may be family, it's highly likely they dampen your life too. Their selfish habits drive you insane. Their demanding personalities tire you. Their condescending remarks make your blood boil.

....

It's true. Old people *can* be grumpy, and we need serious help with how to manage those relationships in a healthy way. Yet before we delve into *why* old people can be grumpy and *how* we can cope, let's be clear—grumpy old people are not grumpy because they are old. They are typically grumpy to start with.

If they are old and rude, there's a high chance they were young and rude. If they are old and demanding, go back in time, and you'll see they were likely young and demanding too. If they like to pick fights with every person they meet, would it be surprising if they used to pick fights with their siblings, peers, and parents too?

It's quite possible you may have had a run-in with an elderly person like this. "Grumpiness" is caused by a variety of factors, but it is not an accurate portrayal of the entire older generation. So remember, grumpy old people are like lemons. Most were a little "sour" to start with.

HOW TO LOVE THE LEMON

The trouble is you know you have to care for this person. If your blood boils or your muscles tense up every time you encounter them, here are three practical steps, based on my personal and professional experience, that may help when dealing with a difficult older person.

1. Understand possible reasons behind their negative behavior.
2. Schedule time for them.
3. Give them grace.

1. Understand Them

One of the silliest things my parents told me growing up was if I didn't finish my food, my future husband would have many pimples. This is a Chinese superstition. Yet for years, I made sure that my chopsticks shoveled every grain of rice into my mouth.

After years of clearing my bowl, I became an adult and, interestingly enough, I married a man who *did* have a fantastic complexion. The one problem I had with him was he wasted way too many tissues. With a father who was an environmental engineer, I was taught not to waste anything. As kids, our dad instructed us to switch the lights off *immediately* after leaving a room to save electricity. He reminded us to turn the faucet off *right* after washing our hands to save water. When we unwrapped a gift, someone always reminded us to unwrap carefully since the paper could be folded and reused.

When it came to tissues, we applied the same guidelines. In our household, a tissue box could sit on our piano for over a month. When I got married, however, Kevin would single-handedly clear a box of tissues in less than a week. As newlyweds, every time he grabbed another tissue, my big eyes bulged. My nostrils flared.

"Can you *please* stop using so many tissues?" I would cry.

Kevin would conduct his usual nose wipe, and then he would grab two or three more tissues.

One year after the wedding, this young wife learned something. When Kevin grabbed a tissue, he actually *needed* it (gulp). A victim of constant allergies, Kevin has dealt with symptoms his entire life. I noticed it when we were dating, but I didn't realize until living with him it was *that* bad.

When it comes to a challenging personality, remember that behind every behavior is a reason. As I got older, I realized there were deep-seated and simple reasons for Yeye's grouchiness. Could this be the case for your situation?

The reality is that "difficult" people often have difficult things going on inside them. As Yeye aged, he became more resistant and harder to deal with. If not for the fact that I lived with him and caught him in vulnerable moments, I never would have the compassion to stick with him; I would have never understood some of the reasons for his rough behavior. If you are dealing with a difficult older person, there is weight and worth to figuring out what could be irking them.

"I wish people knew that elderly people still have strength. That many of them are strong. And strong-willed."

MARY, 85

When we understand why someone is having "lemony" behavior, we gain another perspective, but many other benefits follow: We are more likely to keep our cool. We take our loved one's negative behavior less personally, and our angry hearts are more able to forgive.

So *why* might some older people exhibit "lemony" behavior?

REASON 1: FEAR

Sleeping in the room next door to Mama and Yeye for over twenty years allowed me to overhear not only the after-hour conversations and bickering my grandparents had with each other, it also gave me a front-row seat to their midnight shuffles, their nightly groans, and even their fearful nightmare cries. All this grew more intense with time and penetrated through that wall to the point that I began to feel weighted from their predicaments.

Fear can lead to a lot of anxiety, but it also can trigger difficult behavior. As an older person ages, they field many emotions and fears. Most noticeable is the fact that their life is nearing an end. With a deadline to life, they can feel rushed and overwhelmed and almost paralyzed as they reflect back on their life's impact or lack thereof. Secondly, the uncertainty of when they will die and uncertainty of how they will decline can present more fear. *What will happen to me as I get older? Will I suffer? How much time do I have left?* One thing that makes aging so frightening is that every older adult takes a different path. The fears are real, and at times, they are unexpressed. When your elder is challenging, is there something you sense he or she may be afraid of? When we understand this, we have greater compassion.

REASON 2: SLEEP DEPRIVATION

Sleep deprivation is a simple reason for "lemony" behavior. What happens to *you* when you don't get a good night of rest? Sleep is a basic biological need for all humans. Lack of sleep can lead to fatigue and irritability and also impair concentration.[1] Did you know over half of older adults suffer from insomnia and, interestingly, many older adults are undertreated?[2] Could it be that because of their health, medications, or environment, they are lacking rest? Could their regularly interrupted and already inadequate rest explain their "snappy" behavior? Thus, when older adults are cranky, maybe there's a simple explanation. Maybe they don't get adequate sleep.

REASON 3: BLAME IT ON PAIN

Pain can also cause irritable behavior. When an older person is in pain, it's easy to overlook or dismiss it as lying or simply trying to attract attention. But older adults are constantly experiencing changes, some of which may cause discomfort and may not be visible to the naked eye.

"I think sometimes the attitude change is reflective of a health change, be it mental or physical."

BETTY, 87

Sometimes we become fussy over a small cold sore or a paper cut, so consider how the physical pain older adults experience can affect their behavior. Have you ever yelled because someone stepped on your foot? Or grunted because you ran into the corner of a table? When in pain, people can be extremely irritable. As a result, they may not be able to hold it together. They may not be polite. They won't always speak in a calm manner. Sometimes they may kick, punch, or even yell.

Did you know that nonverbal patients with dementia sometimes will kick and hit as a way to communicate, "Don't touch me. I hurt"?[3] Knowing this, caregivers are less likely to take these outbursts personally because with late-stage dementia, agitation can be an indicator of someone's pain.

One hundred sixteen million adults in the U.S. suffer from chronic pain.[4] Many will tell you how pain not only disrupts their involvement in work, school, or leisure; it also disrupts their relationships with others.[5] What causes "lemony" behavior is also not limited to physical pain. Pain can be physical, psychological, or emotional. Thus, when a person lashes out, consider how it may indicate deeper and more complex forms of pain.

In Yeye's last year of life, he fell and acquired a deep wound that wouldn't heal. As uncharitable as it sounds, he would mention it often, and to me, it sounded like complaining or groaning. While Yeye was known for being difficult, his challenging behavior grew worse in his last year of life. During that year, Yeye snapped at others, hit people, and lashed out in anger. Looking back, I realize the pain of an open wound could very well have contributed to his lack of control over his emotions. If I had known the impact of pain back then, I would have extended more grace and compassion.

Whatever the case, if we want to honor the older adult, we need to take their pain seriously.

REASON 4: THE PAST

A deeper reason for difficult behavior is the past. Traumatic past experiences can haunt a person for life. It can cause people to be more distrustful and guarded. Most noticeably, it can make them more difficult to love. As someone gets older, they begin to reflect on past events. As death becomes real, traumatic memories earlier in life surface. Intense emotions well up in the individual and can be more than they can process on their own. These unwelcome memories are sometimes more than they can contain.

In Yeye's lifetime, he experienced a lot of hardship. He never talked about it, but throughout the years, I had many memories of Mama searching the house to find me. She'd ask me to give Yeye a hug if he was in a particularly sour mood. "Yeye lived a hard life," she'd say. She repeated this often. When he was a young husband in China, Yeye was detained by Communist soldiers. They withheld food and drink from him, held him captive in a dark room, and forced him to apologize despite false accusations against him. After this experience, Yeye's father-in-law helped him escape from China to Hong Kong to avoid future detainment. I can't imagine how terrifying that one experience was. Having no food. Held captive. Forced confessions. And to feel so threatened that he needed to escape.

Even a glimpse into someone else's story gives us greater understanding of their behavior. In Yeye's case, it helped me understand his paranoia, his distrust, and his fighter-like personality.

Though understanding someone's past doesn't necessarily make them easier to live with (oh darn!), it does strengthen our ability to extend more grace.

REASON 5: AN ACCUMULATION OF LOSSES

Mama was always a social butterfly, but as she neared her late nineties, she was no longer interested in going out. When I offered to take her to elderly fellowship where some of her longtime friends were, she declined. In hindsight, I realize that, even if she saw her friends, she couldn't have a meaningful conversation with them. No matter how much she wanted to engage, the loss of hearing and of vision resulted in more isolation and loneliness for her.

Loss can lead to all sorts of negative emotions. By the time they reach an advanced age, older adults may experience an overwhelming number of losses, aside from hearing loss. This can significantly impact their everyday life and mood. Consider the number of loved ones an older person may still, on some level, be mourning—or at least missing—including spouses, parents, siblings, friends, and even children.

"Hardest for me as I got older is that I lost my last brother. It causes you to look back and think: I lost my brother, mother, father, sister and brother.
'Lord, am I next?'"

MARY, 85

In addition to such losses, older adults also grieve the loss of independence, the loss of mental and physical abilities, the loss of their homes, the loss of their belongings, the loss that comes with change, or even the loss that keeps someone from hobbies and activities that used to bring them joy and purpose. Loss has the ability to suck the cheer out of someone's life.

REASON 6: NEEDING HELP ALL THE TIME

It never feels good being the needy one in a relationship. But as people age, they end up needing more help, no matter how independent and strong they used to be.

About ten years ago, when my older neighbor was downsizing and trying to clean out her house, I offered to help her transport unwanted belongings to the local donation center. As I piled a few trash bags into my car, she said, "I'm not used to asking for help so often." To most of us, asking for help implies we are inconveniencing others. When we have to ask for help and ask for it often, it can be humbling, and even depressing.

Remember, when an older adult asks for help, they usually ask because they have no other options. They hate to burden others, so typically they only ask for the bare minimum and end up neglecting a slew of other desires and needs of theirs. This can often lead to internal frustration and negative outward behavior.

REASON 7: THE ABSENCE OF TOUCH

Does the older person you know get affection? When my youngest screams and fully utilizes his lungs, the only way I can calm him is to hold him. Along the same lines, when Kevin and I are on edge with each other, I'd be lying if I didn't tell you a little intimacy miraculously resolves things.

One long-term research study of nearly five hundred adults showed that babies who received the most affection from their mothers had the lowest levels of distress, including levels of anxiety and hostility as adults.[6] As people age, they lose most of their immediate family, meaning they also lose many of the people who embraced them, kissed them, and gave them other forms of physical affection. Affection is a powerful way to feel love, but as people grow older, sometimes the only touch they receive is from hired help. Aging is a tough process, and one that could truly benefit from more hugs.

....

Though these are seven possible explanations for an older adult's unpleasant behavior, there are many others. As you interact with challenging grandparents, parents, or other older folks, make it your goal to hear them out, uncover their story, and learn more about them. In doing so, you grow in understanding as you identify both their triggers and what sparks a smile. As you seek to understand the hard-hearted older adult, I'm convinced you may develop a deeper respect for them. You know, some of the toughest, meanest, snarkiest, and despicable people actually have some of the most interesting, mesmerizing, heart-stopping, and inspiring stories to tell.

Now on to the second practical step . . .

2. Schedule Time with Them

After a long discussion about understanding a person, it seems far too simple that we would only need to schedule time with someone to be able to cope with their difficult behavior. But it *can be* that simple. When you schedule time with a challenging older person, you remind them that they are important to you. The saving grace is that you also set some healthy boundaries. Let's say your dad who is in his eighties asks for help excessively or will only accept help on his terms. His critical spirit may wear at you. Scheduling time for your dad allows you to say, "I'll come every Saturday. I can't help you now, but I can help you on Saturday when I come." This limits the amount of time he may annoy you, but also limits the chance for you to bark back at him.

Setting aside a regular time to help, connect with, or visit your older family member allows you to limit your interactions in order to appropriately manage expectations. It will assure the older person of a time when they'll have your undivided attention. It'll also give you peace knowing that you are showing them love and care.

Clearly, if you don't have a good record with an older family member, it won't benefit either of you to spend a lot of time together. Brief is sometimes better. So start small and do what you can handle. And know that your invitation to meet with them regularly speaks volumes.

3. Give them grace

Whenever you spend that scheduled time with your challenging grandparent or parent, come bearing loads of grace. As people age, they are drenched with loss in all aspects and flooded with various emotions. Thus, older adults, even the nice ones, need a lot of grace.

What is grace? Grace is the special favor of getting a birthday party in July when you already celebrated in May. Grace is when your husband brings you flowers after you vented all your complaints to him. It's unexpected. It's undeserved. Grace is medicine (the good tasting kind) for a grumpy soul.

When my grandma was in her most advanced years and living with my oldest sister, she was unable to eat certain textured foods, so my sister Jo would take special effort to cater a meal for Mama. Sometimes Mama would comb through her food and look around, and then take a small nibble. Clearly, she didn't like the menu that day.

> The fact is, when you serve a difficult older person, you will not get gifts or gratitude in return. But that's the beauty of grace.

Anticipating and knowing that my grandma wouldn't always be happy with her special meals, Jo strategically kept a stash of ice cream in the freezer just in case. If Mama didn't like a meal, Jo extended grace (and ice cream) to Mama, and it always put Mama in a better mood.

The fact is, when you serve a difficult older person, you will not get gifts or gratitude in return. But that's the beauty of grace. You don't need to wait for a certain response; you can give it at any time. The next time an older adult throws their meanest, most stubborn, difficult self your way, let it serve as a signal that they need some grace. And use it as a powerful secret weapon. Buy them flowers. Treat them to doughnuts. Drive them to the calmness of water. And in your own style, surprise that lemon with something sweet and good.

DON'T LOSE HOPE

After twenty-six years of living with my grandparents, I finally had a valid excuse for moving out: I got married! Two days before returning from my honeymoon, I received a voicemail informing me of a sticky situation. For the first time in ninety-seven years, Yeye had a stroke. Ironically, although his speech was slurred and his left side was unbelievably weak, he still put up a fight. First, he refused to go to the hospital. And later, he absolutely refused to go to short-term rehab. In his mind, stroke or not, he was going home. No question about it.

Strokes affect the flow of blood to the brain and other parts of the body. One of the essential keys to recovery is rehabilitation. Needless to say, my dad was panicking and completely at a loss at Yeye's refusal to go to rehab. Mama, at 94, was frantically calling every family member looking for a resolution. Yeye, still lying in the hospital bed, was accusing people of trying to kill him, and stubbornly resistant even to the doctor's order.

As I stood in the hotel hallway that evening listening to my sister's phone message, I heard the words "stroke" and "short-term rehab" and instantly, I knew what had to be done. It's no coincidence that one year earlier, I transitioned from working in the fitness center to the Admissions Department for Riderwood's extended care facility. My main role was to help market the assisted living, skilled nursing, and particularly short-term rehab care.

Maybe it was the snuggles I gave him when I was a little girl or perhaps the many times I drove him to the store after I got my license, but over the years God gave me unique opportunities as a granddaughter to sweeten up my strong-willed grandfather. At times, his selfish and rude behavior drove me insane, but through understanding his behavior, God gave me a compassion and conviction to love Yeye and not give up on him.

At my first chance, I got Yeye on the phone and offered him the option to come for rehab. "It's where I work," I assured him. "And I'll get to see you almost every day." Even over the phone, I could sense his stone-hard demeanor soften in an instant.

As you reach out to the most difficult personalities and persistently try to care for them, don't lose hope in your situation. Bless the hard-hearted person even if they show no outward signs of it. Your love is not wasted.

The truth is, you and I are capable of "losing it." We can be lemons. When my husband does not get hearty food, he gets crabby. When Baby Ben does not get enough Mommy time, he gets cranky. When Silly Sam does not play long enough outdoors, he becomes creatively destructive. When my big girl Maddie does not have any more soft leggings, she gets sassy. When I don't get sleep, exercise, alone time or friend time; when I'm stuck wearing my thick glasses instead of contacts or my hair won't behave; or when I'm hungry, see more dirty dishes, or step on a Lego—watch out world, the mood in the Tom household turns sour fast.

Even when my handsome husband and those adorable faces appear, I glare at them. I shout mean things. I become a lemon.

When I deserve a heavy time-out, what I really need is for someone to remind me that I am dearly loved. The same holds true for the difficult older person. The hard-nosed, grouchy older adult desperately needs someone to remind them that they are dearly loved. They need to be reminded of this over and over and over again. Whenever you're tempted to lose hope, don't forget that behind every grouchy behavior is truly a reason for it. Sour things take a great deal of sugar to sweeten up, so resolve to pour love into the sour people in your life. Understand them, affirm them with your time, give them grace, and then shoot for lemonade.

....

TAKE NOTES | *How to Cope with Grumpy People*

Understanding a person's negative behavior doesn't necessarily resolve it. A lemony person may still throw shots at you, bad-mouth you, or use you. With strong personalities like that, you may not be able to change them, but you can use techniques to personally cope with their behavior. Here are ways to better cope with challenging older adults.

BE READY FOR RESISTANCE

It's important to expect resistance, and more of it as a challenging person's health deteriorates. As people decline, they are internalizing many emotions from illness, loss, and even the guilt of the past. We can expect elders to have hard days as they struggle. I've seen the most gentle people become obsessive about having certain items with them—almost as "security blankets"—as their health declines. Certain behavior like needing things a certain way or in a certain spot may be unreasonable, but the fear of decline and death can be frightening, and where an older adult can maintain control, they will try.

TAKE CARE OF YOURSELF

When you deal with someone who is demanding, self-care had better be at the top of your list. One of the hardest parts about loving a difficult person is that subconsciously they may devalue you. They might criticize the way you cook or the way you raise your kids. Taking care of our own needs reminds us that, despite the way a lemony person treats us, we are still valuable.

So, eat well. Exercise. Spend time with life-giving people. Take small and big steps to do what's good for you. It will take time to figure out a rhythm. And it won't look as ideal as, "I help my mom, and I work out every single day." Or, "I care for my needy grandparent and make beautiful, handmade cards and bake cupcakes for my friends each week." Instead it will look like, "I made it to the gym once this week, and I visited my mom and did not get short with her." Sing hallelujah when you take steps to care for yourself. Doing what is life-giving helps prepare your heart and mind to serve a grouchy person, but also lets you decompress after exasperating moments with them.

REMEMBER YOU ARE THE LAYER IN BETWEEN

Before our emotions reach the public, some of us are blessed to have a spouse, a parent, a sibling, or close friend to bounce our thoughts off of, to vent to. These friends or family serve as a layer in between; they hear us out and help us work through some of our strongest and worst emotions. Therefore, those who aren't as close to us often get a cleaner and kinder message. If an older adult loses their spouse, however, they lose the layer in between; they lose someone to filter their thoughts. Naturally, the next closest people to them take that role of hearing, filtering, and sounding board thoughts. They may not have been informed; they take on that role naturally. Simply put, your grandparent or parent may no longer have someone close to them to process their raw emotions with. Without knowing, this role to manage the older adult's worst emotions may have landed on you. If you find yourself on the other end of very strong emotions, remember you are getting the first draft of their unfiltered thoughts. Understanding you are the layer in between helps you remember not to take their rash behavior personally.

Sometimes a difficult person simply needs an outlet to express his or her emotions. Their social circle is weakening;

their friend base is shrinking. Offering a listening ear is one of the best things we can do for someone exhibiting difficult behavior. If at all possible, when they make comments, don't cut them off, don't correct them. Just listen. At the end of life, especially, we may hear a person complain about physical pain or how they wish they would die soon. Our natural tendency is to say, "Don't say that!" or to refute their words. But let them vent, knowing that inside there are a lot of emotions bottled up and waiting to be processed. They need a sounding board, a person to vent to. We can bless them by taking on this role.

BE STRATEGIC ABOUT VISITS

It's tempting to want to break off contact with your hard-nosed loved one, but we know this isn't always the best option. To cope with your grumpy "friend," be strategic about when you are in contact with them. Choose times when you're feeling your best, when you might be best able to respond in a mature manner. For example, don't answer the phone if you are already stressed. Reserve visits for afternoons if you're not a morning person. Don't text during the late afternoon when you're busy with dinner prep. Don't talk right after work if this is when you are most uptight.

Grace Lebow and Barbara Kane, authors of *Coping With Your Difficult Older Parent: A Guide for Stressed-Out Children*, offer some great suggestions, including to keep visits with a "negative parent" brief.[7] They say that more time with such a person is not always better. If you are visiting from out of town, Lebow and Kane suggest not spending every minute of your visit with your negative parent. Instead, also schedule other activities you enjoy so you are able to care for yourself. Do what you need to do to allow yourself to be the most patient.

PRAY

An extreme personality calls for supernatural help. Get on your knees and trust in a higher power; pray for your grumpy older adults. When at our wits' end, or even before we get there, we shouldn't forget to enlist the help of the One who knows the elder better than we do. God has made this person. God has seen the events from childhood to older adulthood. It's worth asking God for help.

chapter 8

OLD IS HEALTHY

I wanted to run a marathon. But I didn't think I could actually finish one, so instead, I put it on my bucket list. The place where anything that feels far-fetched goes.

Over twenty-six miles (26.2 miles to be exact). I had run races before, but when it came to a marathon, I was tired just thinking about it. Like any sensible person, I asked, "Will I be able to finish the race? Will my bones break down permanently from all the repetition? Will I even have fun doing it?"

Maybe I could attempt this feat later in life.

Some people post pictures of world-class athletes to inspire them. For me, inspiration hit when I met Paul. It was 2006, the time when I worked in the Riderwood Fitness Center. Paul, a petite 84-year-old, came and worked out regularly in the fitness center. At first sight, he was quiet; after I mentioned I had run a few races (shorter ones, that is), the conversation picked up.

A late bloomer, Paul started running at fifty-eight. He was

getting his annual checkup when his doctor broke the news: he needed to exercise. Peering out the window that day, Paul told me he spotted a group of lunchtime runners streaming through the city. "How hard could *that* be?" Paul thought. And that's when he started running.

Rather than slow down, Paul's running picked up through the years. At seventy-one, he ran his first marathon. When I asked him how many he completed in his lifetime, he tallied. "The Marine Corps . . . the Cleveland Marathon . . ." he paused, "Five, not very impressive."

That's out of this world, I thought.

The more we talked, the more impressed I was. Of the five marathons Paul had run, he finished a few under the four-hour mark. My ears perked up; this happened to be a goal of mine (and still is).

Being the runner he was, Paul asked me early on, "Are you considering running a marathon?"

Though tempted to lay out all my excuses, Paul, at 84, left no room for that. "You can do it," he said matter-of-factly. Paul was still a member of a local running club; he was still running. *If Paul could run a marathon in his seventies,* I thought, *I, at 23, could surely attempt to run one.* Right?

And so with bucket-list jitters, in early 2007, I clicked "register" and committed myself (by paying a very high race fee) to running 26.2 miles. *I must be crazy,* I thought.

For the next five months, I religiously followed the Hal Higdon running schedule. I wanted to finish the race injury-free. But behind that, I also knew I needed to train well because I had accountability. Every time Paul bumped into me, he would ask, "How many miles did you run this week?"

As he reported his mileage to me, I would report mine back to him (it was embarrassing anytime I missed a workout). So even when I had no motivation, I still tied my laces and pushed myself out of the door. All because of Paul.

A NEW HEALTHY HABIT

What's your latest health craze? Last year, I was all about eating red onions. I replaced quinoa for rice. I started adding fresh cilantro and basil to everything. I even made recipes with turmeric!

When it comes to health trends, there are many of them. Cut out gluten. Lift weights. Practice yoga. Breathe deeply. Rock climb. Run. Invest in essential oils. Drink green smoothies. Decrease screen time. Don't use plastics. Eat super foods. Go organic. Incorporate flax seeds into everything. Don't weigh yourself. Dance. Laugh. Jump on trampolines. You've heard them all.

Or have you?

Have you heard of this new healthy habit? Spending time with older adults is physically, mentally, and emotionally healthy for you. That's right, spending time with older people is one of the most overlooked yet healthiest practices. Just like with most healthy habits, it's not always easy in the beginning (wheat bread never tastes good when you start!), but the benefits both for you and the older adult community are widespread.

TENDER REMINDERS
TOWARD GRATITUDE

First and foremost, spending time with older adults is healthy because it can teach us gratitude. The Greater Good Science Center at UC Berkley has studied the science of gratitude, and in one of their comprehensive reviews, they say that "gratitude may be associated with . . . better physical and psychological health, increased happiness and life satisfaction, decreased materialism, and more."[1] When we are grateful for what we have, we feel better. Research also shows that in being grateful, we are "less likely to experience burnout," "more willing to seek help for health concerns,"[2] and more likely to experience better sleep.[3]

> *"Celebrate everything in life—nothing is too unimportant."*
>
> **JOANNE, 77**

When older adults are part of our lives, we quickly realize the stark contrast between our lives and theirs. We are humbled as we realize the gift of good health and relationships. We learn to be thankful for everything; we learn gratitude in the gentlest way.

Gratitude for Health

Watching an older loved one's health deteriorate is like letting a five-hundred-pound barbell drop on you. Thud. It is heavy; it is hard. It is sad. On the outside, spending time with older people appears depressing or even unhealthy for our souls, but when we regularly sit in the presence of someone who experiences decline, something beneficial happens.

First, we gain a clearer picture of "whatever is true" in the person's life. This is the heavy, hard, and really sad part. Sometimes it can be funny (like dentures falling out when your grandpa laughs). But most of the time it is humbling, even disturbing. Don't stop visiting, however. Your grandparent, your parent, your older friend needs you.

After being a walking powerhouse for many years, my mood dropped whenever I saw Yeye permanently attached to his walker. It was so *not* him. After having her head buried in delight over reading her Chinese newspaper for many years, my shoulders sunk whenever I saw Mama staring off, no longer able to read because of her deteriorating eyesight.

"I wish people knew how many parts of the body there are that can go wrong when you're aging. Because things deteriorate much more rapidly than you think they're going to. And people age at different rates."

JANE, 86

Because I lived with Mama and Yeye, I witnessed subtle losses they experienced. I saw them struggle to do things they once did with ease. I saw the vulnerability on their faces when they attempted and failed. Watching decline is painful when we love someone, but it's not helpful just to sit in sadness.

While we naturally feel grief, with time, we can grow in gratitude. See, when we serve someone in their decline (and if we stay committed to them) our first emotion is sorrow, but our second emotion can be gratitude. It may feel wrong to be grateful for something which our grandparent or aging parent may no longer have. But think about it: in showing up, you can use your health to make up for your older adults' failings.

THE DECLINE I WITNESSED	FIRST EMOTION	SECOND EMOTION
Seeing Mama sit at a party unable to engage, unable to chime in on conversation	Sadness	Gratitude for the ability to hear
Seeing Mama hesitate at the top of an elevator, fearful she would fall	Sadness	Gratitude for agility
Hearing Mama and Yeye frequent the bathroom in the middle of the night	Sadness	Gratitude for the ability to enjoy a full night of sleep, gratitude for a working bladder
Hearing Mama shuffle rather than walk confidently around the house	Sadness	Gratitude for the strength of my legs
Talking to a resident with dementia who no longer remembered me	Sadness	Gratitude for good memory

Hearing an elder complain about constipation	Disgust	Gratitude for a working digestive system, for healthy bowels
Seeing a nursing home resident bedbound	Depression	Gratitude for independence
Hearing Mama would have to get shots in her eyes for macular degeneration	Sadness/Fear	Gratitude for healthy eyes (even if I have a high prescription)

Yes, "whatever is true" for an older person may very well be slow-moving bowels. This may sadden us; it may even disgust us. But when we observe, listen, smell, feel, and serve those who are growing old, we see their struggles, we sense their sadness, and we get a whiff of the older person's life. This is when true gratitude begins to sink in. Because when someone we love stumbles, it leaves us humbled.

Gratitude for Advances

Interacting regularly with the old also allows us to appreciate the simple things in life. For me, it helped combat entitlement. I grew up in a high-class neighborhood where luxury cars filled my high school parking lot. People sported expensive brand-name watches. Fast food was far too low class. Parents held positions at successful businesses and companies, served as head coaches of professional sports teams, or owned their own large businesses. The rest were executives, surgeons, professors, and lawyers.

Back at home, life with Mama and Yeye contrasted the affluence. Mama sat at the kitchen table and sharpened pencils with a razor blade. When the sun was the brightest, Yeye would clip his clothes on a line to dry. Their beds were made out of cinderblocks, a plank of wood, and blankets for padding. As I reached middle school, I caught on.

My home environment didn't reflect suburbia. It was more like World War II survival mode. We weren't poor, but I was accustomed to the lifestyle. Plastic bags and large barrels were used for extra storage. Yeye had a suitcase full of clothes with some money (you didn't hear it from me) stored underneath the bed. Jars of sugar were hidden behind cloths. And when it came to food, Yeye stored up four loaves of bread, three cases of soda, and jars of coffee, lest he get anxious about being without.

While balancing living in a ritzy area with wartime survival tactics was not easy, it gave me perspective. Have you ever noticed that when you spend time with younger people, you appreciate the things you once had but no longer exist? "Years ago, we used to . . ." A similar effect occurs when we linger around the old. Instead of missing things, we stop taking things for granted. We gain an appreciation for the advances that have come with time.

Gratitude for People

Being in the presence of older adults also teaches us gratitude for our relationships. It's easy for me as a young wife to complain about my husband, but spending time with older adults has stopped me in my tracks. Because many older adults are widows. Some widowed only once, others widowed twice or even three times. What they tell me is that one of the hardest parts of aging is losing a spouse.

"I lost my husband several years ago. They [my kids]
were in their thirties and they were very close to their
father, but they both had lives they went back to.
And they talk about him, remember him. But my life
changed drastically and it will never be the same.
And that's been hard."

KATHLEEN, 70

"What you miss when they're gone is there's no one
to talk to. We did a lot of talking together and
all of a sudden that part is gone."

LEN, 88

When I hear that, it reminds me again to cherish Kevin and not take our relationship for granted.

And just like we shouldn't take family for granted, we shouldn't take friendship for granted either. As people age, I've observed how friendships can become distant because of physical and mental decline. Without transportation, an older woman may no longer be able to visit a friend. Without good hearing, an older woman may not be able to hear her friend.

A few years ago, a former resident of mine, Walt (98), moved to assisted living. He shared, "It would be nice to have more people with whom I could converse. For a while, the people were uncommunicative."

Len (88) also moved to assisted living. I appreciate his honesty: "It's hard to find equivalent people that you can tie something you can call friendship to. It's hard to make friends."

I WANT TO BE LIKE *THAT* WHEN I GET OLD

When we spend time with older adults, we begin to appreciate our health, our material things, and our relationships; this is healthy and leads to healthier life choices. Having older people in our lives gives us a chance to learn, not simply through insight, but through example. And whether elders are fun, happy, angry, greedy, crude, mean, slow, fast, skinny, big, frumpy, and anything in between, we see their examples. We can learn from them.

When people meet my mom, they're always amused.

This year, one year shy of turning seventy, my mom went skiing again at Lake Tahoe. She has her own equipment, and in the past two decades she has traveled to Mont Treblant, Beaver Creek, Vail, Copper Mountain, and Heavenly, just to name a few. Mom has traveled the world, stayed in hostels, and even swum in the open ocean, all in recent years. On the streets, she zooms around in a bright yellow hatchback, watches movies before I get to them, and last year, when my sisters and I tried to schedule a Mother's Day meal with her, she exclaimed, "I know! I want to take you all to Happy Hour!"

"I want to be like *that* when I get old!" peers will say.

Here's a newsflash: You don't wake up adventurous on

your eightieth birthday. And you don't turn ninety and all of sudden turn flabby and fat. If you track back into my mom's earlier years, this is what life looked like. In her forties, Mom joined a master's swimming group and started swimming at the Y. In her fifties, she stopped sitting with all our bags in the ski cabin and took to the slopes herself. In her sixties, she traveled the world. Do you get it? She's always been adventurous.

"I still have some adventurous spirit in me.
And I am not really afraid of many things."

LAURIS, 80

Similarly, when people met Mama, especially in her last few years, they admired and were amused by how, at such an old age, she still had such a grateful heart. She coined the phrase "Thank you very muchie, jie, jie," which means "Thank you very much. Thank you" in "Chinglish." Spend just a few hours with Mama, and it was clear how thankful she was. Anytime someone blessed her, she was quick to thank them. Our family all remembers her for that.

Having lived with her for most of my life, it's no secret to me how Mama ended up brimming with gratitude. Even in years when she sat for entire days, she would sit and would recount aloud how grateful she was for people who helped her throughout her life.

For example, she recounted her father's kindness during childhood when he sent her to Japan to study abroad. She recounted how as a young wife in poverty, a lady gave her shelter and a bowl of rice when she had nothing to eat. She recounted when she was a mom with two little ones, and a young lady helped her carry my aunt, who was only a few months old, as they went from Guangzhou to Hong Kong to meet my grandpa. She recounted how my mom, her daughter-in-law, treated her so well. See, Mama wasn't only grateful in her nineties and hundreds; she always had a grateful heart.

Have you ever wondered what *you'll* be like when you get old? Some things are obvious. Some things, not so much. In general, however, your current behavior often can determine your future behavior. Figure out the pattern for yourself:

CURRENT YOUNGER BEHAVIOR	WHEN YOU GET OLD
If you don't brush your teeth often now,	you will have rotten teeth.
If you listen to loud music often now,	your hearing will be poor.
If you argue and complain a lot now,	you will be argumentative and critical toward those who help you. People will not want to help you.
If you are impatient now,	you will be impatient. As your body slows down, you will grow increasingly frustrated with yourself.
If you are physically active now,	you will be active and will maintain independence longer.

If you eat fatty foods now,	your joints will hurt, you will suffer from more chronic illnesses. Old age will be harder for you.
If you are content with life now,	you will be more accepting and humble. People will enjoy your company.
If you are grateful now,	you will be grateful. People will feel more inclined to help.

Your disposition and attitude today are good indicators of what you'll be like when you get old. If you are disappointed, no need to fall in a puddle. You can be kind, grateful, adventurous, and fun. You just need to start working now to grow yourself into the person you wish to become. It's quite simple.

If you want to be adventurous when you get old, try new foods or experiences now.

If you want to be healthy when you get old, develop the discipline of regular exercise now.

If you want to be content when you get old, practice being content with what you have now.

If you want to be patient when you get old, stop your road rage, your rush and hurry, slow down, and consider others before you rush now.

If you want to be filled with gratitude, start saying thank you, write thank you cards, and offer appreciation to others now.

If you want less wrinkles, moisturize and use sunscreen now.

You Can Still Do It

That's the good news. We can work at being adventurous, healthy, and grateful older adults. Yet all too often, we fall into a trap. We gripe about getting old, believing that the older we get, the more useless we become. We use age as an excuse: We can't start running. We can't go back to school. We can't audition for that play. And we can't contribute. Can't. Can't. Can't. Not when we get old.

> Develop relationships with older adults and you'll gain a more accurate picture of what is possible as you age.

But develop relationships with older adults and you'll gain a more accurate picture of what is possible as you age. The truth is aging does create challenges. Yet all too often we blow these barriers out of proportion. We allow those challenges to cramp the potential of our future selves and those older than us. When we say, "I'm getting old," most of us mean to say that we are growing incapable, simply because of age.

Connecting with elders inspires us to change that mantra. I'm amazed when I recall what some of my old friends did. Len went to law school in his fifties. Mary wrote her first book in her sixties. Paul ran marathons in his seventies. Steve cycles in his eighties. Mama encouraged a recovering friend (two decades younger) at the hospital, and she was in her late nineties. Clara checks in on residents at the assisted living, clips hundreds of coupons for military families stationed overseas, walks about 1.5 miles daily, and bowls with the Wii bowling club, and she is currently in her hundreds.

Our elders provide evidence that we can still accomplish incredible things as the years go by. Sometimes it may require more work, determination, time, or perseverance. But we shouldn't stop dreaming, hoping, and striving to achieve, serve, and contribute. Because even as the years bump up, you and I are still capable.

I remembered when, around the five o'clock hour, my alarm blared. The sky was dim. The birds were chirping. I fought to keep my eyelids open. It was race day! I ate my Luna nutrition bar (a morning run routine of mine), changed into the running outfit I had placed out the night before, and like a crazy person trekked down to D.C. (still not completely awake) to do something I'd never done before. On that October day, for the first time in my life, I ran and ran and ran. After downing tons of sports drinks, taking bathroom breaks in the bushes, and waving to thousands and thousands of lively fans, four and a half hours later, my sore and salty legs passed the finish line. I had done it. I completed the Marine Corps Marathon.

One full day of rest and recovery (ice baths, eating, and sleeping) later, I returned to work. Like usual, first thing in the morning, I checked my inbox. There was an email from Paul. "Congratulations," the subject line read. "I checked your times online," Paul wrote. Then he added, "I think you can run faster." Paul's challenge dumbfounded me. Wasn't that enough? For a few months, I rested. But as the next year rolled around, I strapped my running shoes on again, pushed myself out the door, trained for months, and like a crazy person gave another shot at the Marine Corps Marathon.

....

TAKE NOTES | *Being Life-Giving Greenery for an Older Person*

When I left for college, I was the last grandchild, not to mention the favorite grandchild, out of the house. With no children around, a cold mood ushered into the home. Yeye became more hostile. Mama was needier and more anxious. The void left by the moving out of grandchildren was a dramatic change that negatively impacted everyone's moods. While I was away at college, Dad encouraged me to call home often. "When you call, your grandparents are in a better mood," he'd say.

As we watch our grandparents or older parents struggle through physical and mental decline, they may need assistance with handling their physical care, but just as much they will need someone around who can help boost their mood.

In the world of home décor, interior designers will tell you that putting plants in your house is life-giving. Floriculture studies show that by simply placing greenery in a room, it can help improve one's mood, concentration, and memory; it has a calming effect on people and can lower stress too.[4]

When Mama and Yeye's motivation waned or their social

connections fizzled, as a young adult, I realized that I could talk to them, drive them to the grocery store, or take them to visit a friend. By simply being around, my presence served as "greenery" that could improve their moods. Whether you take your older friend out for a meal, bring your older relative flowers, or simply work on your laptop next to them, these are ways we can serve as a live plant in their spaces.

....

chapter 9

BUILDING A VILLAGE

It still gives me tingles when I think about how a village came together to care for Mama.

In the last month of Mama's 102-year-old life, her daughter flew in from Canada to be with her, her daughter-in-law handled paperwork for her nursing home stay, her grandchildren coordinated shifts to keep her company, and great-grandchildren cheered her up with cards, pictures, and songs. Her 80-something-year-old brother even traveled five hours for a short visit where he simply held her hand. Between family and friends, we kept her warm water refilled, cooked her favorite soups and fed her, helped her to the bathroom, and made sure a blanket always kept her warm. In those last weeks, a village beautifully came together to serve Mama. And she was so blessed.

Most of us know the value of having a village when it comes to raising a child, but can you sense the value of having a village to care for the older person too? Caregiving is a huge job, one

149

that is not meant to be done alone. Statistics show that "more than one-fifth (22%) of caregivers are exhausted when they go to bed at night, and many feel they cannot handle all their caregiving responsibilities."[1] If you have watched exhausted parents or been involved in caring for an older person yourself, you know the job you're up against. Caring for an older person can be physically tiring, emotionally draining, brain-cell blowing, and more. That's exactly why we could all use more help.

When recruiting more help comes into conversation, however, the comment I often hear, mostly from burnt-out adult children, is that older parents—even the easygoing ones—voice their preference to only have family help them. "I want *you* to do it," the aging parent will say. And while this sounds like a heartwarming idea and is the most commonly practiced, it neglects to accept the truth that caring for an aging person is a far bigger job than most of us imagine. Sometimes in attempting to provide our aging relatives with the best, we find ourselves panting from simply doing the basics. And this is exactly why we need a village. We want to provide our elders with the very best loving care, but we will fail miserably if we do it alone.

Building a village goes far beyond getting more help; it comes down to our own well-being and survival. With little or no support, caregiving can lead to serious health consequences. Study after study reveals that caregivers show higher levels of depression, stress, and frustration. Physical health is negatively affected. They have increased risk of heart disease and lower levels of self-care. When we care for others (whatever age they are), we are better off to have a village, one that can help carry the load, one that can back us up.

The Family Caregiver Alliance calls caregivers "a population at risk," where caregiving-related stress led to a 63 percent higher mortality rate in elderly caregivers (aged 66–96) compared to non-caregivers at the same age.[2] Yes, caregiving may even lead to a faster death. The fact is, without a village, we harm our physical and emotional health; we harm the well-being of our elders too.

> *"The hard parts of taking care of a baby seem manageable because you know that it is only for a short time, and then in many ways, it gets easier. But caring for an aging relative usually doesn't get easier. It gets harder and harder. And then they're gone. So my only advice is to be gentle with them and be gentle with yourself."*
>
> **AMY, 39**

With all the negatives related to caregiving, it may be tempting for us to bail out and let other family members or even professionals take on this hefty job. But you and I all know that, at least in the case of family members, this is not a possible option (I mean, our parents would kill us!). In all seriousness, leaving our elders be is probably the worst choice. Emotionally, they'll feel totally unloved. Physically, their health will be negatively impacted. Then we'll forever feel guilty. And when they're gone there will be no going back either. We will be sure to feel regret.

That's why, if we want to do ourselves and our elders a

favor, we need to strategically love our elders. We need to build a village.

OUT-OF-THE BOX BUILDING

One of the reasons Mama had such a large village surrounding her in her last years of life was because over a decade earlier, our family experienced an unexpected turn of events, the type that sparked some out-of-the-box building. While I was in my senior year of college, my dad experienced some health issues and my parents considered moving closer to Dad's work. Two days after my college graduation, my parents, after living in our home for almost thirty years, found a new place and decided to sell our childhood home. Never recalling a move in my life, it took some time for the shock to set in. A few days later, something else happened that shook things up. My sister Jo and her husband, Jason, looking to gain a better commute and more space for their growing family, decided to buy our childhood home from my parents. And if that were not enough to jolt a mini heart attack in me, Jo and Jason came to my family and proposed a generous but strange idea. Would Mama, Yeye, and I want to stay in their home?

Their offer shocked me. But can you imagine at 21 how ecstatic I was that I wouldn't have to live with my parents anymore? My grandparents were also relieved they didn't have to move. They wouldn't have fared well in a completely different environment (most older people don't). When it came to my parents, they were humbled by the generous proposition.

By then, Mom and Dad had lived with my grandparents for almost three decades, and in the last four years an underlying tension rested in our home. Mama and Yeye were still fairly healthy in their nineties, but in those four years with no grandchildren around, their lack of motivation and purpose caused them to be more emotionally needy; there were no grandkids to give them attention. This drained my parents and, in the walls of their own home, they were unable to rest.

Jo, who was married but still lived close by, made it a point to visit home weekly. When she did, she saw my parents troubled as they tried to manage the emotional needs of Mama and Yeye—their anxiety, fear, their need for attention. This convicted my sister to help.

Thus, in their late twenties, Jo and Jason invited my grandparents (and me) into their new home and started what became a thirteen-year journey as primary caregivers for my grandparents. They became the sandwich generation, a term to describe those caring for children and aging parents, only they had extra layers of bread in between. They courageously opened their home to the elderly with little knowledge of the drama and joy that lay ahead. This was out of the box, but this was the beginning of something beautiful.

HOW TO BUILD A VILLAGE

Should you want to build a village, or at least a stronger one, the first thing to remember is you have to be creative. Unintentionally, a unique living arrangement (housing those from ages 0 to almost 100) forced our family to find unconventional ways to serve Mama and Yeye. Jo and Jason, in particular, were posed with the challenge of entertaining, managing, and pleasing people from polar sides of the century. While handling school drop-off, lunches, permission slips, appointments, and activities (not to mention homework or emotions) for four children, Jo and Jason also catered their lives, meals, and schedules to support aging grandparents.

And though they had compassion and youthful energy to offer, their job was far from easy. For example, they needed to keep the babies safe, but if they used baby gates this would restrict 90- and 93-year-olds from easily getting around the house. They also wanted to let my grandpa do his own thing, but that meant a blaring TV that prevented the possibility of early bedtimes. They struggled to balance and meet everyone's needs. But through Jo and Jason's generosity, an intergenerational dorm life on overdrive evolved, one that allowed me to see how much bigger, stronger, and more fun a village can be.

If not for the years I lived with Jo and Jason's growing family and my grandparents, I might have always assumed a village was only comprised of adult children. In that case, I would have simply suggested that people birth more children as an insurance policy for the later years. Population growth, activate! But with a new perspective, I realized something: if we want to build villages that engage, support, bring joy, comfort, and love to our elders, we need to open up the doors to our villages and invite more people in.

Now every village that surrounds an older adult will look a little different. Each will include a unique crew of people all able to meet the needs of the elder in a different way. Some may serve more; some may serve less. Some may serve as chauffeurs; others may serve as cheerleaders. Some may handle the bulk of managing healthcare; some may simply greet with a cheerful smile.

As we build our villages, the most important thing to remember is that every person in a village can help in a different way. In his book *The 5 Love Languages*, author Gary Chapman talks about how quality time, words of affirmation, gifts, acts of service, and physical touch are different ways we express and receive love in the context of marriage.[3] In the context of caregiving, however, these various ways of communicating and receiving love paint a picture of how an elder benefits when there is a *village* versus *one person* caring for them.

Let's look at a village that is caring for an elderly woman and see how she benefits from a bigger support system. One person may spend time sitting on the porch with her (quality time). Another person may shower her with words like "I love you" or "You're doing great, Mom" (words of affirmation). Another may bring her flowers or a memento from their last business trip (gifts). Another may schedule her doctor's appointments and drive her there (acts of service). Finally, another may give a

> As we build our villages, the most important thing to remember is that every person in a village can help in a different way.

hug or hold her hand (physical touch). Imagine. If this woman only was loved in one way, she would be missing out. Right? The bigger the village, the more capacity we have to bless our elders. The healthier and happier they become.

Unexpected Villagers

As I mentioned, I cannot overemphasize the importance of opening up our doors to create a bigger and, more importantly, stronger village. In line with the fact that everyone has a different way of connecting and blessing our older relatives or friends, I want to spend the rest of this chapter talking about some villagers that are sometimes overlooked when building your village.

GRANDCHILDREN: THAT'S A SUPERPOWER

To me, watching grandchildren love on their grandparents is like eating crispy hot nachos oozing with melted cheese. It's so satisfying. Why? Because some grandchildren have discovered that loving their grandparents is not as stuffy as it sounds. They've invested in their grandparents and have discovered something special about it.

For the person blessed to still have a living grandparent, you must know that you have a unique ability to bring joy to the older person like *no one* else can. You have the ability to speak life into an older adult, which I consider to be a superpower.

It's an unspoken expectation that adult children take care of their parents, but when it comes to grandchildren, it's natural to be confused about what our role should or can be. There are parenting resources. There are grandparenting resources. But people have not thought about the grandchild's role enough for there to be resources, much less a term to describe the grandchild's role. In fact, you might call this book, the first "grandchilding" resource in town (can we patent that?).

All this is to say that grandchildren have been completely overlooked and underutilized in the task of caregiving, which to me is incredibly absurd considering the impact grandchildren have on their grandparents. Have you ever observed the look on a grandparent's face when they hold their first grandbaby in their arms for the first time? Have you ever observed a once strict parent throw discipline out of the window and spoil their grandchild silly? Have you ever stood by a giddy grandparent as they bombard strangers with stories of every move their grandchildren make? They get into others' personal space and say things like, "Isn't she *so* cute? He is the smartest kid I know." It should go without saying, then, that grandchildren have a way with their grandparents.

> For the person blessed to still have a living grandparent, you must know that you have a superpower.

> "Being a grandma. I think it's the best job in the world."
>
> **LAURIS, 80**

If you've ever wondered why the grandchild/grandparent relationship is one of the most fun and peaceful in the family unit, it's because there is less baggage in that relationship. Just consider how rocky parent/child relationships can be. Throughout the growing and adult years, parents and their children constantly wrestle for control. As the child grows up, the parent holds on. As the parent declines, the children grow frustrated. All throughout the relationship, both parties often manage to injure each other. Multiple times.

In contrast, the grandparent/grandchild relationship is often smooth, filled with more grace, fun, snuggles, and, very likely, more gifts. That generation in between does wonders, doesn't it? For this reason, grandparents often are less resistant to grandchildren than they are to our parents. And this is why grandchildren shouldn't be forgotten in the village; grandchildren need to know they have a superpower. Consider: if something important needs to be said to an elder, maybe grandchildren should be the messengers. Due to the nature of the relationship, the elder may be more open to listen.

Aside from convincing my grandpa to go to short-term rehab, when I convinced Yeye to designate and sign the power-of-attorney form, something he refused to do until he was 97, my dad was overjoyed. If anyone mentioned this form, he would accuse them of wanting him to die. But when I approached him, he obliged. My success didn't result because I cared more for Yeye; with a generation in between, there was simply more grace and less tension, so he would listen. Grandchildren can bless without baggage.

In our family's village, grandchildren added a strength

that mattered, especially when the unexpected hit. In 2013, my dad was diagnosed with a rare form of cancer. During the two years that Dad was enduring treatment, my sisters and I teamed up to care for my parents, but also to care for Mama. When you witness a loved one's body being invaded by deadly cancer cells, sometimes you struggle with how to help. Subconsciously we recognized that when someone is sick, they worry about their own health, but they also worry about their obligations. The painful reality was that our dad's health was declining at a faster rate than his elderly mother. In caring for Mama, we gave Dad peace knowing in the present and future, his mother would always be taken care of. Throughout Dad's battle with cancer, this was a significant way we honored him. A month shy of Mama's hundredth birthday, Dad passed; our family continued to care for Mama, knowing that more than ever, she would need her village.

NONRELATED YOUNG ADULT: A PERFECT FIT

Naturally, you may be inclined to create a village only comprised of family, but don't rule out those who aren't related. Many grandchildren (maybe you're one of them), whose grandparents have since passed, would be more than willing to serve an older adult if given the opportunity. Since my mom was caring for Dad, and my sisters and I all had young children, sometimes even after brainstorming complicated schedule arrangements, we were at a loss as to how we could keep Mama company. Eventually, this forced us to ask for outside help. Over the last two years of Mama's life, there were amazing young adults, both single and married with kids, who were so kind and eager to keep Mama company when the rest of us couldn't. It took time for her to get used to them, but in time, Mama became comfortable and content when they were around.

> *"As you get older, you can't do as much as you used to, so being able to say to someone, 'Here's a list of things to do for me,' would be great."*
>
> **HELEN, 65**

When you take a look at places like Riderwood, you can see how even those nonrelated can be some of the best people to recruit for your village. At Riderwood, you can walk into the dining room and see practically as many students as you see older adults. High school and college students are in record number serving as cooks, cashiers, servers, hostesses, dishwashers, and the like. It's not the typical crowd you'd expect at a senior living community, but it adds a sweet flavor to the place. Residents thrive because of it. They recognize students and often call them by name. They check up on them or ask them a slew of personal questions. Sometimes they add a joke and laugh, or they offer their unsolicited "two cents."

Though in the early years of the company, people warned Erickson that highschoolers wouldn't be able to hold it together, he still embarked on a signature program that he now calls "one of the greatest values of the company."[4] Residents treasure student presence so much that many of them contribute to the community's student scholarship fund every year. Riderwood now offers $1,500 scholarships per year to students who qualify, and this is solely funded by residents, who not only appreciate these students but are proud of them.

Whether it's asking a young man to pick up Grandma for church or asking a young lady to keep Mom company, don't rule out the teenagers, the college students, and young adults. They've got something to give.

CHILDREN: WHAT ABOUT BACON?

People underestimate the ability of older adults; they also underestimate the ability of children. When Mama was in her sitting years, her great-grandchildren took small parts to bless her. Julia helped fill Mama's pillbox. Jonathan helped prepare Mama's early morning breakfast. Josiah reminded her what the day of the week was when she asked. Jubilee held her hand annually when she got a flu shot.

Much to some people's surprise, their little hands made a real difference. When Mama was 98, though she was still fairly independent, it became apparent that preparing breakfast was becoming dangerous. Because Jonathan was the only other early riser in the house, Mama would ask him for help. He'd grab her mug and help her fill it with hot water; then grab an empty bowl and her Ensure shake from the refrigerator. In first grade, Jonathan learned how to use the stove, and so while Mama mixed her coffee and instant oatmeal at the table, Jonathan would be cooking eggs and sometimes bacon for his breakfast.

Whenever visitors would come over, Mama would gloat about how her great-grandson helped her in the mornings. "He's *such a good boy*," she'd repeat over and over in Cantonese.

Seeing that Jonathan was so helpful, Jo formalized his good

deeds and began paying him fifty cents to encourage Jonathan to continue helping his Tai Paw, which means great-grandma in Cantonese. If I was at their house extra early, there were times Jonathan would be sitting on the top step right below Mama's room waiting for her to wake up. One morning in particular, around 6:30 a.m., Mama must have eyed Jonathan's hot breakfast because he ran up to my sister, still sleeping, and whispered, "Can Tai Paw eat bacon?"

BABIES: SUPERPOWER ON OVERDRIVE

My family likes to joke that with each great-grandchild Mama had, it added another year to her life. Even without a formal study, I know this is true. By the time Mama turned 102, she had ten great-grandchildren and she spent considerable time with almost all of them. She'd carefully inspect their small fingers and admire their infant hands. She'd sniff and savor the smell of their fresh skin. She just loved having children around. When I slept over when my sister's family went on travel, Mama always requested I sleep in the bed next to her and reminded me to bring the baby, tears and all. "I'm not bothered by crying," she would say.

"Most of all, I wish people knew, always take the older person to your children's birthday party or what activities your grandchildren are having because grandpas and grandmas and elderly people love little children."

MARY, 85

This is the ridiculous truth: babies don't even have to lift a finger to bless an older person's life. They eat, poop, sleep, and cry (boy, do they cry), and immediately old heads pop up to catch a glimpse of this little life. If you want the easiest way to bless the old: let them see, feel, hear, and hold new life. Let them do it often. It does wonders. Without a saying a word, babies possess a superpower on overdrive.

PROFESSIONALS: DO WE REALLY NEED THEIR HELP?

It's highly challenging to foresee the future needs of older adults. At some point, their health will take a downturn, but we rarely know how or when. As a result, when their health fails, it's possible that you or your home may not be equipped to care for your elder. I had always promised (like many families do) that I would *never* move my grandparents into a nursing home. Never. But after a debilitating fall, Mama's health required 24-hour assistance and after tiring attempts to care for her at home, our family realized we couldn't care for her on our own. Moving Mama to a nursing home was heart wrenching, probably harder than saying goodbye. But after moving her, I gained an appreciation for nursing home staff, particularly the aides.

If not for the help of the nursing home aides, our family would have exhausted ourselves caring for Mama's physical needs and would have neglected to spend time cherishing our last days with Mama. Having the extra help allows us to focus on spending quality time with our elders, which is the most important thing we can do when we know someone's time is short.

But sometimes we are reluctant to hire or recruit professional help because we don't want the elder to feel abandoned. What we need to remember is that professional caregivers are not replacing our village, they are simply becoming part of it. We are adding them to our team. This is something we can tell grandparents and older parents when they accuse us of abandoning them or when they're resistant: we involve more people only because this allows each of us to be more refreshed and to offer the best care.

But hiring caregivers, bringing in other senior care services, or recruiting hospice is not just about getting help with the physical tasks; it's about giving us space so we can step back and process the sad reality that plays out in front of us. On the outside the more we serve our elders, the more we internalize this lingering reality: our loved one may not have much time left with us. Once you know someone is nearing death, the very best thing to do is to cherish the time you have left with them. Those memories will stay with you a lifetime. But the truth is, if you don't have extra support, you will miss out on being present during the final moments.

THE PERSON WHO NEEDS
THE MOST SUPPORT

We need to build a village around the elder, but there is someone else who needs a village too—the primary caregiver. Grandchildren, nonrelated young adults, babies, and professionals are important parts of a village, but they are rarely the ones in charge of an elder's care. The person in charge, also called the primary caregiver, carries most of the load. As a result, they're often the most tired.

When we watch the primary caregiver, we think: Is it possible to evenly distribute all tasks among family members or villagers? Ideally, that would be awesome. Logistically, however, it would a nightmare. If everyone took on the same exact amount of responsibility, confusion such as whether medications were refilled or taken or changed at the last doctor's appointment would be bound to occur. Thus, having someone oversee all care is advantageous.

It *is* unfair that the primary caregiver typically puts more time and effort into caring for an elder. In the five years after college when I lived with Jo and my grandparents, I saw the big and small ways Jo served Mama and Yeye. It was a lot. That's exactly why I offered my help whenever I could. If my grandparents weren't feeling well at night, I willingly responded to their calls. If they needed a ride to the store or to elderly fellowship, I was glad to help. During that time, while I was in my early twenties, I saw how appreciative Jo was to have an eager and dependable villager.

Thus, when I moved out and had a family of my own, I still offered to help Jo care for Mama. I knew how much she appreciated the support. I also knew she needed it. Did she need someone to stay with Mama? I'm there! Did she need someone to clean Mama's laundry? I got it! Does Mama's hair need to be washed? I'm your girl!

Whether it's your sister or your parent who serves as the primary caregiver, remember they need help. By being a backup, respite, and support to them, you bless them. You also extend their life as a caregiver. Dr. Williamson, in *Keeping Love Alive as Memories Fade*, said this, "You'll get a bad attitude if you never get a break."[5] Thus, when Mama was nearing 100, I (along with my supportive husband) offered to sleep over and stay with Mama to allow Jo and Jason to take a family vacation. With three young kids of my own, it wasn't a walk in the park to haul our family over and attend to Mama's needs, but we knew Jo and Jason needed a break, not to mention personal family time.

By caring for the primary caregiver, we build a better and more sustainable village, which naturally leads to a happier elder. So remember to treat the primary caregiver well. Eagerly volunteer. Offer them respite. Bring them gifts. And learn to be a good listener. They have a hard job on their hands. One that requires time, strength, patience, and a whole lot of love. When you offer support as a right-hand man or woman for the primary caregiver, *that* will make a world of a difference. Just ask them.

THE WAY CAREGIVING WAS MEANT TO BE

Do you ever hear of violence, addiction, child loss, or abuse and find them extraordinarily heartbreaking? You don't see any good in it. Aging often feels the same, doesn't it? We watch once-healthy people grow frail and helpless, and that sadness overwhelms us.

In working in the aging and end-of-life care field, I'm all too aware of how once-healthy people grow frail and helpless. When I witness this heart-wrenching process, I'm not going to lie, my heart sinks all the way down to the solid concrete bottom, whether I know the person or not. Watching someone's health deteriorate stinks.

As the heaviness of aging may at times make my heart sink, there is one thing that always brings me joy. It's when, amidst the trial, I see an eager and attentive village racing from all directions to love the older person. This is when I see hope. On our own, we can only do so much. But with a village, we carry and uplift an elder during the hardest of times. We team together and bring good to a heavy situation. And that's how our village came together for Mama. We showered her, spoiled her, served her to the end. And she was healthier and happier because of it. This is the way to honor our elders. This is the way caregiving was meant to be.

....

TAKE NOTES | *How to Use Your Superpower*

If you're looking for ways to activate your superpower as a grandchild or young adult, here are some meaningful ways to sweeten up the life of an older person:

LET THEM SHARE THEIR STORY.

Adult children have heard their parent share the same story (or joke) over and over again. They share these stories because they cherish them, but it can become background noise for their children. As a grandchild or young adult, bless the older adult with fresh ears. Ask them about their life. Listen eagerly to their jokes. And let them enjoy telling that story over and over again.

SHOW INTEREST IN YOUR FAMILY HISTORY AND DOCUMENT IT.

Patricia, a mom and the oldest grandchild in her family, was not close to her grandfather growing up. Interested in learning more about their family roots, she asked her grandpa on a recent trip about their family tree. His eyes lit up. This convicted Patricia to document her grandfather's life. She arranged to interview him over Skype and was surprised when he came well-prepared, sheets of paper in hand. Last Christmas, Patricia was able to present her grandfather with a sixteen-page document called "Slices of Life." As you can imagine, he was honored. You can do the same.

ONE MINUTE CHECK-INS.

If you're a busy person, know that short visits can be just as effective as long ones. Older adults know young people are busy, so when we take even a minute to connect with them, they appreciate it. Call, text, email, send a letter, pop in, give a kiss and a hug, and in doing so, we remind our elders they still matter.

TRAVEL WITH THEM.

One 80-year-old said it best, "Many older people would travel if they had someone to go with them." Bless your grandparent, parent, or older friend with a travel companion. It will give them comfort knowing that if they are sick or have an accident, someone they know can help them.

....

chapter 10

TAKE ADVANTAGE
OF THE SWEET SPOT

Villages come together when crisis occurs, but let's say your grandparent or, more likely, your aging parent is healthy. What do you do then? Do you twiddle your thumbs until that first episode hits? Or kick back until someone needs assistance? Far from it. When your elder or "elder-to-be" is healthy, you need to know that this a prime time in your relationship. This is a sweet spot for you to gear up and prepare for the hike ahead.

In the eight and a half years I worked in the hospice field, I learned that there are things we can do to make that hike easier. In my role, I managed and developed end-of-life education for both community members and health professionals. Though I didn't directly serve dying patients, I was close enough to hear far too many instances when suffering occurred, when someone did not have a gentle or peaceful ending. In the hospice and palliative care profession, you quickly learn that many crisis moments like suffering, family drama, and high levels of stress can be avoided. In taking certain steps while a person is still healthy or at least still communicative, the stress can be decreased to a much more manageable level. What we do now sets the stage for a much more pleasant caregiving experience, for the elder and for us.

HOW IT'S DONE

According to my definition, the sweet spot is when an older person is still in fairly good health. By this, I mean they're able to get around and are independent. No serious health condition has hit. The sweet spot can also encompass times when the older adult is experiencing good health in the short-term—maybe they're in between hospital visits, surgery, or a health lapse. It represents a time when an elder is feeling their best.

When we take advantage of this sweet spot, we cherish the good times by being intentional in *how* we spend time with the older adults we love, fully aware that it impacts their quality of life later.

> *"You do want them to care. You do want them to think, 'How can I serve Mom? How can I serve Dad? What can I do at this point?' But you don't want them to be overreactive; you want them to be servants and caring, but not worriers."*
>
> **HELEN, 65**

Build Trust

The best way to take advantage of an older adult's healthy years is to start building trust in the relationship now, and to make it a priority. Why? Because caregiving in hiking terms is classified as a "difficult" hike. It requires a great deal of energy, effort, and perseverance. In every step of your hike, trust is like quality hiking boots and trekking poles. It makes all the difference, especially when you hit steep inclines like tragedy or disease. Trust makes all the difference when difficult decisions need to be made.

Trust, however, also takes time. And this is where we often fall short. We get in the routine of managing an elder's physical care and forget to nurture that relationship. We forget how important trust is in the caregiving journey. But that's why it is so important to build trust before health declines. Because when health diminishes and difficult conversations and decisions arise, our grandparents and aging parents will be far less anxious and resistant if they can trust you. If they can't, it may feel impossible to help an elder when hospital visits or health issues become reality. During those times, your older relative may question your motives and offer more resistance. Breaching discussions about future living arrangements or care may be a challenge.

Do yourself a favor and find ways to build trust in your relationship with your elder now, when they're feeling their best. When an elder trusts us, they know we're on their team. When an elder trusts us, it comforts them knowing they have someone to depend on. When an elder trusts us, they know we have their best interest in mind. They can feel stronger and more secure going into old age. We can find compromise and work through tough conversations with far less resistance.

If you don't have a good relationship with a parent or grandparent, however, building trust may seem far from attractive. Maybe your parent grates on your nerves and their acts may seem unforgivable, but I encourage you not to give up. Some family situations are almost impossible to reconcile. But even so, put effort into building a stronger relationship with a parent or grandparent, however poor your relationship is. In the end, you'll have a clearer conscience knowing you tried; you'll have more peace, especially when your older relative dies. For you, building trust may take more creativity, energy, and time. It may come in the form of short phone calls, cards, or regular financial assistance. It may mean you love intentionally from a distance.

The key is that you still love. And if you can't muster up love for your parent's sake, then honor your parent or grandparent for the sake of your children (or future children). Because one day, don't you know, *you* will be the old person who needs care. And if you want your kids to take good care of you, then someone has got to show them how it's done. Loving for the sake of setting an example is a worthwhile endeavor.

Create Good Memories

One of the best ways to build trust, even in a difficult relationship, is to create good memories. But the key is to do it now. Because good memories are far easier to come by when an older person is healthy. It's also much more fun.

"In my mum's healthy years, I loved taking classes in the community with my mum. We took all sorts of short courses together like cake decorating and flower arranging. We even volunteered together."

TANYA, 42

Especially if they are in their fifties, sixties, or seventies, take my advice and plan a vacation with your parent or grandparent. Spend memorable moments together when everyone can still enjoy themselves. Buy those cruise tickets. Visit those national parks. Take a bus to the city. Plan a fishing trip. Go, go, go!

When your parents or grandparents are healthy, *this* is the time to do things together. *This* is where you'll find some of your most treasured memories. Realistically, in a few years, you may want to plan a vacation, but by then it may be too late. Physically, your elder may not be mobile or healthy enough to travel. Mentally, they may not feel comfortable in new places or certain scenarios. I've talked to active older adults who are anxious about trips because sleeping in a different environment causes extreme sleep deprivation or getting to bathroom facilities soon enough on a plane is a real concern. So don't postpone vacations. Go on vacation and create good memories now. Take advantage of the sweet spot.

In the book, *Mended*, Blythe Daniel and her mother Helen McIntosh write about restoring the mother-daughter relationship and suggest some other ways to strengthen a relationship. They suggest: "Find the common ground between you and celebrate it. . . . [T]he key is to find it, accentuate it, and to invest in it with her."[1]

Your common ground could be sitting over coffee or bubble tea together. Your common ground might involve shopping. Maybe it's talking sports. Whatever it is, invest the time and money into doing things with the older person. Good memories will pile up and then the blessing of trust will too.

Find Out What They Want

Whenever I hear of siblings in conflict over their elderly parent's care or hear deep regret from adult children questioning whether they made the best decision for their parent, I can't help but think how much drama and heartache could have been prevented if the older adult had communicated their wishes early on.

Let's say we were eating lunch together and while I was in the restroom, the server asks *you* to order for me. How would you feel? You'd probably feel uncomfortable making the decision for me. I mean, what if I never told you I disdain mushrooms? I'm guessing you'd feel nervous if I wasn't happy with my meal. You'd probably feel fine, however, if before I went to the restroom, I told you exactly what I wanted.

Making food choices for someone else is already difficult. Making decisions regarding someone else's *care* is ten times more of a struggle. Even though they love their parents, adult children naturally feel guilt, fear, and anxiety making decisions when their parents are no longer able to. They don't know enough information regarding what their parent's preferences are. Goodness, they never talked about it.

And we can't assume we know what someone else wants. I remember a fellow health professional sharing how she assumed both her parents would want to die at home. She expected this because in her culture, dying at home was the norm. When she finally talked with her parents, however, she was shocked. Her mom, to this daughter's surprise, actually wanted to die in the hospital; her dad then had very specific requests of where and how he wanted to be buried. Until that discussion, she had no idea!

Straight up, if you want to be confident in how you care for your elder, find out what they want. Talk about it. Of course, if you have any experience caring for an older adult, then you know that talking about future care is nothing like discussing a food order. But that's exactly why we need to take advantage of the sweet spot; we need to discuss what an older person wants *before* their health declines. When you find out what an elder wants early on, you set yourself up for easier discussions, less trauma, drama, and pain; you put yourself at an advantage.

This is the reality. When someone is in the midst of trial— maybe they've just received a diagnosis, or they're in the hospital or a rehab facility, waiting for the next step—they are often the most vulnerable as they are flooded with conflicting emotions; they may waffle about their preferences too. Naturally, they're not able to process as clearly as they typically would. They're more easily triggered and more anxious. In contrast, if you ask someone to make healthcare decisions when they're feeling good, they can make more rational and reasonable decisions for their future.

The rule of thumb is: the sooner you talk about their preferences regarding the future, the better.

ENCOURAGE THEM TO MAKE DECISIONS WHILE THEY CAN

When we find out what our elders want, we can encourage them to make as many decisions as they can while they're healthy. Then, they're more likely to have peace with the outcome. Len, one of the residents I used to work with, and his wife had a positive experience moving into a senior living community that we as grandchildren and adult children can learn from.

"We (my wife and I) had both been ill, and when we were better they (his son and daughter-in-law) said to us, 'We don't do very well with long distance illness. Please come and move here and pick your own place to live, so we don't have to come and find a place for you.'"

Len's son and daughter-in-law handled the situation well. They encouraged Len and his wife to choose where they'd want to live. By letting an older adult make their own decision, *your elders* are happier because they get to choose what meets *their* needs. By letting your elder make a decision, *you* also feel better and have more peace about their care.

The unfortunate reality is that if your aging relative doesn't make their own decisions, someone else in the future will have to make those decisions for them. And it won't always be in line with their preferences.

Talking about aging-related issues is hard. It's important to realize, then, that these conversations are not meant to happen all in one sitting. Realistically, they may occur within snippets of conversation, or they may occur over several heart-to-heart talks. Maybe years of them. The hardest thing is to start the conversation, but you might be surprised, just like the daughter I mentioned earlier, to hear how many thoughts your elder actually has regarding future care, housing, or end of life. Aging and the possibility of death are on an elder's radar; in my experience, many seniors are often relieved when they have the chance to talk about the process of aging and their thoughts about it.

WHAT IF THEY DON'T WANT TO TALK?

Because discussing death is a real challenge for adult children and even health professionals, I want to address the question: What if an older person doesn't want to talk about the tough things?

You, of all people, are aware of your parent or grandparent's reluctance to talk about certain topics. It may be culture. It may be personal. Whatever the case, recognize that these difficult topics only get more challenging to talk about with time. Take the time to think through a long-term strategy on how to broach these conversations or research other strategies to address those topics. It is necessary.

One warning in broaching these tough topics: don't fire away with questions. That can scare anyone. Some of my former hospice nurse colleagues have shared that if a parent seems resistant to talk about difficult decisions related to caregiving, a helpful approach is to work it into other conversations.[2] That's genius. In fact, sharing other people's aging-related circumstances and using that as a conversation starter can be immensely helpful. It's much less intimidating, and you can draw out a great deal about your parents' values this way. For example:

"It's interesting that Judy's mom wanted to be cremated. I know you like to save money, Dad. Would you do that?"

"My coworker was talking today about his mom who recently moved to a retirement community in California. It seems really nice. Would you rather live close to family or is weather more important to you?"

"Mrs. Smith ended up getting a feeding tube. I learned that feeding tubes can often cause a person to suffer if they are at the end of life. Would you want a feeding tube if you were in the same circumstances?"

"That was a beautiful memorial service. What did you think of it?"

If your parent is uncomfortable talking about the future directly, consider yourself an investigator. The more you know about your elder's preferences, the more equipped you are to make decisions for your elder when they are no longer able to. The more you learn about your parent or grandparent's preferences, the more comfortable and confident you will be to advocate for them.

> The more you learn about your parent or grandparent's preferences, the more comfortable and confident you will be to advocate for them.

Realistically, your parents may not be ready to talk. Kip Ingram, the Director of Bereavement Care at Montgomery Hospice, located in Rockville,

Maryland, works with many families after the death of a loved one, and he offered this important reminder, "If you initiate conversation and your parent doesn't want to talk about it, you are not a failure."[3] Sometimes we beat ourselves up when our elders won't talk about important topics that could benefit their future care. There is no need to feel guilty. Make the attempt. And if there is resistance, wait a little time. Then, bring it up again when the time feels right.

GET EVERYONE ON THE SAME PAGE

Getting everyone on the same page helps reduce a lot of the chaos and drama when a senior's health fails. To start, encourage your parent or grandparent to fill out an advance directive. An advance directive documents in writing what that person's wishes are at the end of life. They are put into action when a person is no longer able to make a decision for themselves. When an older adult fills out an advance directive, make sure all family members or key village members know about it. And although documents like advance directives are important, be sure to have Mom, Dad, Grandpa, or Grandma verbalize what they indicated on that form (most importantly, who they chose to make healthcare decisions for them if they are unable) and share them with everyone.

Why is it important to do this early on? Because as Dr. Shahid Aziz, author of *Courageous Conversations on Dying: The Gift of Palliative Care*, writes: "One's capacity to make decisions can be lost in a flash from trauma and disease."[4] Especially when someone is in their later years, tragedy could happen at any moment. If everyone in an elder's village or close circle knows what he or she wants, the more advocates he or she has. The better safety net the elder has to ensure they receive the care they want.

Discussing end-of-life issues is just as, if not more, important as documenting them. Why? Because when emergencies happen and documents are not available, Emergency Medical Technicians (EMTs) are encouraged to resuscitate patients, whether people want this or not.

Here's the reality: an advance directive is paper and will not always save you. A voice will.

On the morning of Yeye's death, my grandpa was living in a small group home setting. Within a week, his health took a downturn. That morning, I talked to him on the phone, and though I was told he wanted to talk to me, all I heard were heavy breaths. I panicked. A few hours later, he was completely unresponsive, 9-1-1 was called, and the EMTs began to resuscitate. They were unable to reach my parents. Next, they called my sister, Jo, who was at work. Jo knew from discussions with Yeye that he did not want CPR done if a situation like this arose. Yeye, at 98, knew what he wanted. The EMTs couldn't find the DNR (do not resuscitate) form, so they started performing CPR. Once they reached my sister, however, my sister adamantly declared, "My grandpa's wishes were that he did not want to be resuscitated." She knew Yeye and could be his advocate.

The EMTs stopped.

The more people who know what an elder wants, the better. The less suffering that needs to occur. Remember this: An advance directive is one safeguard to ensure a person's wishes are fulfilled. Family and friends are the other safeguard. But to be an effective safeguard—to be a good advocate—you *have* to know what your loved one values and wants. You also need the major players in the village to be informed. Otherwise, this is where family drama begins.

Do your family and your elder a favor by finding out what your aging relative wants. Find out what they want to "order." Find out what they want when it comes to their care. Because you can't advocate for someone if you don't know what you're advocating for. When an elder's wishes have not been shared with everyone in their close circle, when everyone is not on the same page, the end of someone's life is chaotic rather than peaceful.

SAY THE FOUR THINGS

Early in my hospice career, I heard Dr. Ira Byock speak and became a fan of his book, *The Four Things that Matters Most*. In this book, Byock shares four phrases that prepare both dying patients and loved ones for a more peaceful ending. As Byock writes: "I've lost count of the number of times I've met people in my office, an emergency room, or a hospice program who have expressed deep regret over things they wish they had said before a grandparent, parent, sibling, or friend died."[5]

Sometimes we can foresee death is near; other times we really can't. If you want to build stronger relationships at any stage of life, especially with those nearing the end of life, consider using these phrases. You won't regret it:

Please forgive me.
I forgive you.
Thank you.
I love you.[6]

How much stronger would our relationships be if they were covered with forgiveness, appreciation, and love? When you are able to say all these phrases to your elder, then, when they are dying, you can have peace knowing it ended on a good note.

TIME IS TICKING

When our aging parents are healthy, we often sense no urgency to build trust, create memories, or discuss and plan for the future. Yet building trust, creating memories, and finding out what our loved ones want is the smartest, not to mention the easiest way, to prepare for the future of our elders.

If you still plan to wait for the first health episode before starting your caregiving preparation, let this statistic sink in. The average life expectancy in the United States is currently 78 years of age.[7] Did you know you probably have much less time than you thought? Based on trends, how much time do your parents have left? And how much time do *you* have left with them?

Take it from me. None of us can predict when death will

happen. People often tell me I've got longevity in my genes. Yeye lived to 98. Mama made it to 102. What people don't know is my dad died at 69. He didn't smoke, he exercised daily. He only ate sweets in small controlled portions. In the midst of battling cancer, I remember hearing him say, "I thought I would live longer." I sure wish he had.

Mom or Dad, Grandma or Grandpa may not be seriously ill or bedridden, yet as Byock says, "We are, each one of us, at every moment, a heartbeat away from death."[8] This is truth. And all the more reason to take advantage of the sweet spot.

....

TAKE NOTES | *Take More Pictures*

You probably have loads of pictures of your dog, your kids, or even your last meal, but do you have pictures with your grandparents, parents, or older friends? Taking pictures with our loved ones is so simple, yet time and time again after a grandparent or parent has passed, I hear people say: "I wish I took more pictures with them!" Pictures are perfect ways to capture memories we have with our older family members. Pictures are also one of the best ways to affirm and remind older adults that we love them.

Take advantage of your elder's sweet healthy years by snapping many memories of them alone, but also with family and friends. Even better, consider hiring a professional to take shots of your family, capturing the precious relationships between the elder and their family. Lifestyle photographers are pros at making everybody and everything look amazing. This is key because older people sometimes feel unattractive and unworthy of being photographed. Let the professionals bring out the best in them. Then, print the pictures out and give them to the elder (even framed!) as gifts. Let those photos serve as visual reminders that they are loved. Let those pictures be a memento that reminds them of their relationships.

chapter 11

HER SITTING YEARS

After Yeye died, Mama, in her late nineties, stopped doing many things she previously enjoyed. She handed the knitting sticks back when I placed them in her lap. She stopped calling friends, mainly because she couldn't hear them (nor could they). She declined going to the elderly fellowship, which she used to get giddy over. But the biggest disappointment came when she stopped reading the Chinese newspaper. This was one of her favorite ways to pass time, but with failing eyesight and months of holding the paper literally an inch away from her face, one day Mama put the paper down and didn't pick it up again. After that, her days were characterized by sitting.

When it came to sitting, Mama had one signature spot. Her black Ikea recliner chair which sat in the living room. It was right by the front door; there was also a large window she could look out of. Nestling her bottom in the chair, Mama would prop her bony legs up on the matching ottoman and in that position she would rest for the majority of the day.

As Mama reached 99, then 100, then 101, I watched her do less and less and sit more and more. There came a point where I couldn't help but wonder how much longer she'd have to sit around. Her life now seemed quite . . . useless. Sitting in her black Ikea chair, Mama occasionally verbalized this same sentiment. With a sigh like a tire going flat, she'd grieved over how she needed help with *everything*. "I'm so old. I have no use," she would say.

....

If you've witnessed old age in someone you love, chances are, you understand. A friend of mine is convinced she wants to die by the time she turns seventy; she is fine with old age, but if her health is not intact, she doesn't see the point. Maybe that's how you feel.

Let's be honest—deeply ingrained into our minds is often this belief that without good health, we're useless. So we praise the older folks who look great or who are active "for their age." We look up to the elder (who for the time being) has overcome the effects of aging. Once they start looking "old," however, and their health declines, subconsciously we're no longer impressed, and we deem them useless.

"Even though I'm older, I'm still useful."

SIU-CHU, 73

You know, our society doesn't spend time with people it considers useless. Just visit a local nursing home and look around. Or better yet, count the number of non-professional visitors on the front desk sign-in sheet. The numbers of sign-ins won't match up to the number of residents in a facility.

DOES GOOD HEALTH = VALUE?

Early in my career, I would never have admitted aloud, but I preferred to work with the healthier older adults—the sick ones made me nervous. I mean—they were sick!

Two years after working in the fitness center, I started working in the assisted living, skilled nursing, and short-term rehab facility at Riderwood. I was starting my master's program at the University of Maryland, and I wanted something new. Seeing that the position involved mostly marketing and didn't require a lot of direct contact with residents, I felt comfortable with this new job.

Naively, I didn't realize that I'd come one step closer to weaker and frailer people. When I stepped out of my office, people weren't exercising like they were in independent living. And rather than walking, many residents were mostly sitting down. I saw more wheelchairs. And there was a lot less action than in my previous job. To put it politely, it was more peaceful.

The most unsettling part of my new job was reading the census. The census is a big deal in senior living facilities. It records how many "beds" are filled on any given day; it also offers a general sense of what is going on health-wise for residents. For instance, it shows when someone is admitted or discharged, whether it is a move, hospital visit, or short-term rehab stay. To stay on track of what was going on in the building, I, along with other staff members, needed to review the census every morning.

The census, though simply a record, became more than just an email to me. It was the first time I had to face the reality of decline. Personally, I hadn't really witnessed decline, as Mama and Yeye, in their mid-nineties, were still healthy. But when I read the census every morning, something happened—I began recognizing names. When Mr. Smith, who I had seen a year ago at the fitness center, moved into assisted living, I saw it on the census. When Mrs. Smith was discharged from the hospital back to rehab at our facility, I caught sight of that too. But the most traumatic moments were when I recognized a familiar name in the "death" section. Every time I did, the blood in my body stopped flowing and I had to pause for a moment.

That type of experience jarred me off paper too. Take the day I shadowed a Riderwood nurse on her rounds at the hospital. Going into a room, I vividly remember walking into a scene I was unprepared for. Instead of recognizing a name on the census, this time, I recognized a face. It was Ron, one of my favorite residents. He was always respectful and kind, but the reason I was fond of him was because of the way he treated his wife. Like many other residents, Ron cared for a spouse with dementia. Often I would see spouses grow flustered with their partner, but Ron was so kind. He'd bring his wife in to exercise and, when he did, he was always gentle; he still looked at her with admiration.

But now, Ron lay in a hospital bed. My shoulders slumped. Just a year ago when I last saw him, he had been so healthy!

When he saw me, delight washed over his face. "Isabel," he spoke in a hoarse voice, "it's *so* good to see you." When he reached out his hand from the hospital bed, I held his hand briefly and gave it a gentle squeeze.

Seeing Ron and other seniors slow down is how I became more acquainted with sickness. The most intimate look came when Mama and Yeye were in their last months, then weeks, then days and hours of life. When it happened, I didn't back away as I might have imagined. I stayed close, probably because I didn't think of Mama and Yeye as frail: I thought of them as people. In witnessing decline from a distance and up close, this is what I've learned: a person's health should never determine their value.

Most of us are blind to the disparities between healthy and unhealthy people until we begin serving and loving someone who is sick. The longer I serve older adults, the more I see how our brains and hearts have excluded our most vulnerable citizens from love. We treat people who are sick very differently. We say, "What's the point of spending time with someone if they're no longer healthy or mentally aware? What's the point of someone if they lose their health and can no longer contribute? They might as well be dead. Right?"

> In witnessing decline from a distance and up close, this is what I've learned: a person's health should never determine their value.

Parents of children with complex medical issues and disabilities know this is a lie. They speak out and fight for good education and healthcare because they know their children, even with trachs, leg braces, wheelchairs, and feeding tubes, are valuable. In the process of caring for their "sick" children, parents profoundly experience how strong, kind, brave, life-giving, and loving their children are. Parents of children with disabilities know how valuable their child's life is, so they speak out because they want their society to recognize this too. Whether it be a child or an older adult, we as a society have to recognize that health status does not determine value.

Sick vs. Dead

Strange though it may be, I happen to have a favorite cemetery. I like it because it's gated and has beautiful, expansive fields of greenery. The grass is always cut evenly; flowers are removed once they shrivel. It's a peaceful and calm surrounding fit for remembering someone.

Recently, as I visited this cemetery, a shocking feeling of familiarity came over me. *This place reminds me of a nursing home.*

I shivered. The more I thought about it, the more it became apparent how accurate I was. At the cemetery, you typically see only a few visitors; those visitors usually don't stay there long. At the cemetery, visitors often bring flowers. In a week they wilt, and the maintenance staff will throw them out.

Walk the halls of a nursing home and the sight is unfortunately almost the same. You only see a few visitors. The visitors typically don't stay long. Family and friends bring flowers and maybe picture frames too. In a week, the flowers wilt and the frames get dusty. Both places are most highly frequented on the holidays.

Isn't it odd how we give the *same* amount of attention and time to people at cemeteries and in nursing homes alike? It shouldn't be this way. People in nursing homes are still with us, and though their health is going downhill, they need us. When someone's body is failing, whether they are in a nursing home or not, they still need our attention and time.

Stick with Them

If we really love and value our older friends, we cannot care for them only when they're healthy; we have to stick with them until the very end. In fact, instead of shying away when older adults get sick, we should be upping our game. Shocking, right? Granted, it can be scary and uncomfortable seeing someone's health diminish. But when health is failing, this is when Grandma, Grandpa, Mom, and Dad need us the most.

If I had to tell you the most significant lesson I learned from my eight-and-a-half years working in hospice care, hands down it would be this lesson: dying people are *real* people.

"I love cake."

SARAH, 71

On the outside an older person's body may be failing them, but inside they still have an active and living soul. They are human. They have a name. They have a family. They still have favorite foods. They are hoping, wishing, and dreaming too.

When Montgomery Hospice, my former employer, admitted a new patient, a clinician would always ask, "What's important to you?" With the limited time they had left, these are the types of responses people had:

Some want to spend time with family.
Some want to make sure their beloved pets are okay.
Some want to be able to continue working.
Some want to make it to their grandchild's graduation.
Some want to be around to see a grandbaby be born.
Some want to make it to tea every Tuesday with friends.

The list goes on. When people are shutting their eyes and no longer sharing sentences, it may seem as if they're already dead. Yes, their body may be inactive, but their minds are still moving. This we cannot forget.

HER SITTING YEARS

In the final years of Mama's life, she wasn't doing chores around the house. Instead, she sat like a champ in that black Ikea chair and for hours on end. Like most caregivers, I tried to encourage her to exercise. But my attempts were hopeless. If I tried to engage Mama in ten repetitions of bicep curls (without the weight), Mama would do one repetition to appease me. Then, she'd rest her arms on her lap and start talking. If I called her out, she'd giggle, and with a giant grin, declare, "The thing I hate most is exercising!" And then she'd keep chatting.

Ironically, in the years Mama slowed down, our family and

friends came to love her even more. If you know an elder who has lost heart because they're no longer active, let them know that just because someone is inactive does not mean they are ineffective. Mama proved this to be true.

SO VERY THOUGHTFUL

When you have a weak body, it's hard to imagine, but you can still bless others by being thoughtful. Though she didn't care for physical activity, Mama used her time to think about others. Even in old age, her mind kept marinating.

Two things that Mama often got on our case about was dating and our eating habits. Though she always was concerned about her grandchildren's relationship statuses, as Mama grew older, she was even more on top of it. While sitting in her chair, she'd signal me to come over. And then she would ruminate over any grandchild who still wasn't married yet. In a serious tone, she'd say, "She's never going to meet anyone! Her church is full of *old* people!" And then like any concerned grandma would, she'd start problem solving. "Can't you introduce her to some nice boys?" Sometimes she'd ask to call my aunt or another cousin to make "arrangements." A week later, or sometimes within the same day, she'd bring up the same conversation again. Behind the matchmaking was a grandma who in her sitting moments cared for her grandchildren.

Besides the dating, Mama was also aware of our eating habits. This is a very Chinese thing to do and how she cared for us. Even with her weak eyes, Mama noticed when my sisters and I, as young moms, fed our kids, but still had plates full of untouched food. She'd get on our case about that. If one of our husbands hadn't yet arrived to dinner, she'd remind us to save some food for them. Even when friends came over, she was attentive to whether they had enough to eat. She'd poke me under the table and whisper, "Do you think she had enough?"

One would think that once you can't get around anymore, your life is over. But even with a limp and swollen legs, Mama sweetened our lives by using her time to think about others. She was not physically active, but, boy, was she thoughtful. And in her sedentary years, became surprisingly more perceptive to the needs of others. What a great example she was.

ALERT!

Yeye, with his keen eyesight and that huge fog light, was the watchdog when he was still alive. But when he passed, Mama sat in that black Ikea chair, and she kept tabs on our family just the same.

During the day, as she rested in her chair and periodically looked out the window, she was the first to spot the mailman and would yell, "The mail is here!" until someone picked it up. She was the first to spot me or any other family member when we pulled into the driveway. Then, she would limp over to the door and open it. If an unfamiliar car pulled into the driveway, she would alert everyone in the house too. Talk about a personal alarm system. All guests benefited from Mama's watchful eye because before they rang the doorbell, we'd already been notified to open it.

Mama was just as watchful when it came to our babies. When each great-grandbaby was in their crawling season, they would crawl around the living room floor. Worried for their safety, Mama would yell "Mommmmeeeee!" anytime they neared the stairs. And anytime she saw a baby doing anything remotely dangerous, Mama was sure to alert us. Ironically, she had macular degeneration, a disease that causes vision loss. But she still used the vision she had left to be helpful. And she definitely was. When Mama kept tabs on us, she reminded us in the frenzy of our young lives that we were loved. What a gift!

A STABLE PRESENCE

She may have been really old, but Mama in her last years also served as a stable presence in not only my life but the lives of many. Not because she did anything tangible for anyone, but because she was always there. Literally in her being home all the time, she brought a strong presence to my sister's home. Call her moral support.

Every morning after breakfast, Mama would hobble over to the living room. She plopped dangerously into her black Ikea recliner chair, and it rocked backwards as if the chair would fall over. Around 9 a.m., it was time for school. As Jo's kids rushed by Mama's chair to put their shoes on, Mama would pat their backs, watch as they gathered their backpacks and lunches, and then, waving and smiling, she'd send my sister and the kids off.

After school, as the kids ran home, Mama would spot them out the window and watch them run up the front stairs to the home. Every time the kids ran inside, Mama was sitting in her chair, always there to greet them. She loved watching the frenzy of backpacks, lunchboxes, and shoes thrown off. She'd yell "Gwai Gwai!," which meant "good boy" or "good girl," as they scurried past her. Then as the kids made their way into the kitchen to devour snacks, Mama pushed herself to standing and teeter-tottered following the trail of kids to the kitchen. She'd sit down right next to them and, by tapping the table, the kids knew she wanted them to share their snacks.

The experts in child development will tell you that children need stability in their lives to thrive. In sitting in that chair and rarely leaving, Mama's great-grandchildren, who were ninety to a hundred years younger than her, came to love Mama as she was a stable and ever-present adult in their lives.

THEY'RE DOING SOMETHING

When someone is sedentary, we assume they're doing nothing; they're inactive. But when someone is sitting, they're rarely only doing that. So much more is often happening. Just consider: they could be observing, worrying, remembering, pondering. They might be reflecting, wondering, listening, hoping. They could be devising, planning, resting, praying. In Mama's worn-down Ikea chair, I'm sure she was doing *all* of that.

Sometimes it may appear that elders have been relegated to sitting. But in sitting and sitting and sitting, they are blessed with long periods of reflection. So, though it may look depressing at times, I'm convinced when our elders are in their sitting moments, the wisdom we so often speak of is developing. The beauty of the old is blooming.

"When you have faith, it's not as bad."

CLARA, 102

The problem is that so much wisdom stays inside many of our elders' minds. Those of us who are lucky get leaks of it. But because many elders are alone, no one benefits from their wisdom. It makes me wonder how many sitting older adults have the capacity to love and shower wisdom on those around them yet don't have a village to bless. If only a village would be smart enough to serve them.

A HALL OF FAMER

Sometimes people think that old people, especially the weak ones, have nothing to give. Yet in Mama's sitting years, she became a Hall of Famer in our book. Every single one of her children and grandchildren, and even great-grandchildren, came to dote on Mama's sweetness. She was the beloved "oldie" of the family. We loved her so. One of her great-grandsons, Josiah, even brought her in for a show-and-tell of sorts—he brought her to kindergarten for 100th Day.

When she passed, it was clear both in the tears and the memories that in Mama's sitting years she was ever so effective. As for her great-grandchildren, most of them were too young to even know her when she was in her active years. It was in her "inactive" state that she blessed them.

For a school writing assignment, my oldest niece, who is now a teenager, wrote an essay to remember her Tai Paw (great-grandmother). Read and see that even people who are sedentary can have a profound impact on our lives:

Why Is Tai Paw Special to Me?

JULIA

Tai Paw is a very special person to me. She is my great-grandma and lived with me almost my entire life. Before she passed away, she was able to celebrate most of my birthdays with me and my family. I am the first great-grandchild, and she knew me the best. Tai Paw was able to meet all my cousins and siblings.

When I was younger, I liked to make origami boats and balls with her, or see what she could create with paper. When she needed help, she would call me by my Chinese name. Every time that she needed warm water, I would go help her fill it up. She always said thank you for everything I did. She loved to have company over to our home and never liked the house to be quiet. If me and my siblings were downstairs playing a game or watching a movie, we would always tell her where we were before she would get worried. She loved having family over and watching us kids play together. When I would practice piano and she was sleeping, she loved hearing the music that I played. When I would wake up in the morning, I would say good morning to her. She would ask me what day it was, or what time it is, all the time. Even if it would get me annoyed I would still try to do it with a happy heart.

One memory that sticks out to me is my ninth birthday. She got me my first watch. My mom asked her what she wanted to get me and she said she wanted to get me a watch. She knew that I didn't have one yet and wanted to get me it. She didn't have to, but she knew that it would be special. It was a very special gift that I got and I enjoyed using it. My mom took me to Target to pick it out and when I saw the light blue and green watch, I knew it was the one. It was a very special watch that I still have today.

I get to share something very special with Tai Paw. On my thirteenth birthday, Tai Paw passed away peacefully. We were able to visit her about two hours before she passed away. I am the first great-grandchild, and that was a special moment that I got to spend with her. It is very special to me since I was able to see her before she passed away. Now when it is my birthday, I get to share the special day with her for the rest of my life.

....

"Are you crying?" my daughter asked me as I silently read this piece. I was moved by how Mama's presence profoundly impacted not only myself, but the lives of so many others, just like Julia. In the go-go-go society we live in, she didn't do very much. But in her sitting years, Mama showed how, as Loren Shook and Steve Winner, authors of *The Silverado Story*, put it, "the human spirit glows until we take our last breath."[1]

And this is how I describe Mama's life. Her spirit glowed until the end. The more I think about it, Mama in her last years became someone her family could rely on. She didn't need to do the dishes or babysit or cook up a meal for us. She just sat with us, offered us her presence, and our lives were better because of it. Her sitting was enough.

TAKE NOTES | *Why Visiting Nursing Home Residents Is More Important Than You Think*

Many people assume that if someone lives in a nursing home, there's staff ready to help the person at all times. Sadly, this is not the reality. The reality is nursing home staff are often overworked and have a large number of residents to care for at one time. They don't have enough time and attention to provide the best quality of care for every individual they serve. The average nursing home staff to resident ratio is anywhere from one staff to 9–14 residents on weekdays and one staff to 10–17 residents on weekends. Each state has varying minimum requirements. Some states only require nursing homes to have one aide per twenty residents.[2] Thus, nursing home residents often don't get as much personal care and attention as we all would hope.

Sometimes we cringe over the thought of visiting a nursing home, yet visiting a nursing home is not simply about just saying "hello" to a grandparent or parent. It can have greater impact than you might imagine.

VISITING CAN PREVENT ELDER ABUSE

Elder abuse is much more likely to occur when a nursing home resident does not have visitors.[3] Overworked with too many residents, staff may neglect to attend to the needs of certain residents over others because they know no one is there to take notice. Residents may also experience abuse from other residents, which is now recognized as more of a problem than abuse inflicted by staff. Whoever the perpetrator, residents with few or no visitors are easy targets for elder abuse, simply because no one is around to defend them.

A few years ago, an assisted living manager shared with me how she caught staff stealing furniture overnight from a resident's room. Many times we don't realize that elder abuse is not simply neglect, but it may come in the form of financial exploitation or physical abuse. According to the National Center on Elder Abuse, women, those with dementia, and those with low social support are at higher risk of elder abuse.[4] In visiting your loved ones at facilities, we create a safer environment for them.

VISITING CAN IMPROVE QUALITY OF CARE

A social worker with years of nursing home experience once told me the sad truth: residents with the most visitors usually get the most attention. When staff see visitors, subconsciously they feel more accountable to provide a higher quantity and quality of care.

The more visitors, professional or nonprofessional, a resident gets, the more sets of eyes are looking out and monitoring their care. It's true. Visitors don't just provide companionship, they also serve as advocates so the resident can receive better care. Even without clinical experience, when you visit a nursing home resident, you may notice their needs or even a change in their behavior. You can serve as a voice for a nursing home resident.

Not only do you serve as a voice for the elder you are visiting, sometimes you end up helping others while you are there. For example, when visiting my grandma at the nursing home, my daughter, only 5 years old at the time, was outside of my grandma's room when she heard the resident next door calling. The staff and I in my grandma's room didn't hear any-thing, but running to find me she cried, "That man just fell!" Indeed, the man had fallen off his bed. Because of Maddie, this resident, alone in his room, probably would have had to wait quite a while for help. But the facility staff came much sooner because my daughter picked up on the urgent need of the man next door. Even if we're not long-term advocates for other residents, we provide an extra set of eyes to look out for an elder. Sometimes we don't have to be trained to help; we simply need to be present.

chapter 12

WHAT AN HONOR

Anyone who cares for an older adult's needs can probably attest to the fact that it can feel like a burden at times. By the time I reached my twenties, that's exactly how I felt about my grandparents. I was tired of living with them. Partly because they were getting in the way (partly because none of my friends were doing it).

At my age, living with old people was not the norm. The norm was thinking about grad school and moving out on your own. The norm was thinking about relationships, the forever kind. The norm was working long hours to prove yourself and moving up the corporate ladder. The norm was also chilling with friends and hanging out late at night. The norm, however, was *not* living with your very old grandparents. The norm was *not* driving old people to the store or to the ER. The norm was *not* shouting because the person next to you was hard of hearing. Or repeating phrases because your dear grandma could not remember. The smothering and attention, the constant asking of questions, the blazing fog light. It was getting to be a little too much.

Meanwhile, I was in the phase of young adulthood when life was all about transition. Friends were moving away for grad school; others were accepting out-of-state job offers. Some were flying overseas to teach English, and, of course, a few of my friends were chasing love (googly-eyed) over state lines.

With transitions all around, I found myself attending a fair share of send-offs. The best ones had food, lots of friends, and a time of sharing. When it came to sharing, everyone started cheering, "Speech! Speech! Speech!" and laughter would erupt. Often, the departing friend would share his reflections over his time in Maryland and also share what he was grateful for during his time in our city. Next, friends would give warm wishes and sometimes share a funny story here and there. We often prayed over the person leaving, and that was a great way to end the night.

THE BEAUTY OF GOOD SEND-OFFS

Good send-offs, whether in airport or party fashion, have a way of making someone feel special. They ease our fears as we move on. Practically speaking, they also offer closure, the chance to reflect, to appreciate others, and the chance to say goodbye. It's a bittersweet celebration.

And there I was attending send-offs as if it were my job, when one day, it hit me: my grandparents were only steps away from leaving—they needed a proper send-off.

Every single white-haired and wrinkled adult needs a send-off:

They need a send-off to remind them they are loved.

They need a send-off where their life can be celebrated.

They need a send-off to commemorate their time here on earth.

They need a send-off where they can share their worries and concerns.

They need a send-off where they can reminisce.

They need a send-off so they can say goodbye.

They need a send-off to see everyone who loves them and to be reminded how pretty darn special they are.

They also need a send-off so they know that they are loved when they venture off to their next place. For older adults, the future can seem uncertain. Even if they know where they are going. And *especially* if they don't.

> ### "I don't want to be a burden. I hope it doesn't happen."
> **LEN, 88**

I was struck. For so long, what appeared to be a burden or the lowly task of helping the old was actually an honor. And I finally caught on: God was giving me a divine assignment, a really noble purpose, to accompany and care for my grandparents as they approached the gates of heaven. As a grandchild, I was actually a chosen escort, one responsible to send off my grandparents and to do it well.

That's why from then on, rather than live a typical busy life of my own right next to Mama and Yeye, I had this desire to send them off with pizzazz. To love them so so so much. To smile at them whenever I caught their eye. To kiss them and hug them really tight. To make them feel less of a burden even if serving them was inconvenient. To intentionally call them to see how they were doing. To find out what was on their mind. To treasure them and cherish them. Once I remembered that I was divinely "assigned," that changed everything.

Accept It or Deny It?

Before you start planning an elaborate send-off, you need to know that the key to planning the celebration of a loved one's life is that you first have to accept that the person is leaving. This sounds obvious. But this is where friends and family seem to fall short; they avoid the reality of death. They deny the reality of the departure. They steer clear of it. They don't want to talk about it. It terrifies them. Even if anyone—a professional or an elder himself mentions it—they refuse to discuss the "d" word for fear of making it happen. Denying death is our first instinct; it's natural and common, but it's harmful in the long run.

A NEW JOB: SERVING THE DYING

For a long time, I didn't accept, talk, or think about death at all. Then in 2010, after two years of working in short-term rehab and walking with Yeye through his stroke recovery, I accepted a job at Montgomery Hospice (hospice cares for people near the last months, weeks, or days of their life).

Granted, at 27, I was not so hot about working in a field related to dying, but my mom highly recommended I branch out and try something new. Whenever Mom "highly recommended" things, it didn't mean she thought it was a nice idea; it meant she was convinced.

And that's how my outlook on death and life completely changed. I now had a job, a unique one (at least for my age) where I was learning about death: the process of it, the ways to care for someone who is dying, the physical, emotional, and spiritual parts of it, the grief that results. And while I assumed this would be terrifying, working in a field about dying was much more intriguing than I'd ever imagined.

Within a matter of months, I wasn't just learning about death, I started experiencing it in my personal life too. Four months after I started working in hospice care, Yeye died unexpectedly. Within the next eight-and-a-half years that I was still working in hospice, Dad and Mama died too. When your work revolves around the topic of dying and you feel the reality of it in your personal life, there's little space to run away from "whatever is true." Ironically, this was a blessing. When my family was dying, I had to face reality.

Take this from my professional and especially from my personal experience: our entire families are better off when we accept and think about death. Because while we can't plan the timing of when death occurs, we do have some control over how painful or peaceful it will be.

It pays to take a look at what happens when you avoid death and when you accept it:

WHEN WE AVOID DEATH

Avoiding death is like procrastinating. Just because you don't think about the deadline doesn't mean it won't happen. Even if you distract yourself with something more exciting, your due date still remains. When you avoid a deadline, 100 percent of the time, it only makes things worse. Death is the same. If you choose to avoid it, it doesn't mean it won't happen—it only means you won't be prepared.

"At my age now, you want to find out how to make a graceful and good exit."

ERNEST, 75

When someone is dying, you cannot treat their symptoms in the same way that you did when they were healthy. Their systems are shutting down and are no longer functioning like they used to. Thus, the usual type of care you're used to, or that most doctors would prescribe for a healthy individual, will not be effective. You cannot feed someone to make them better. You cannot force air into their lungs and expect it to be as helpful. You cannot expect forceful pushes on their chest to resuscitate a person. The treatments used to cure a healthy body don't work as effectively, or at all, when a person is dying. Specialized care is needed; this is the best time to call in hospice services. But if you don't acknowledge death is coming, you won't be able to get that help.

Because we, as family and friends, have such a hard time confronting death, sometimes we rob our loved ones from getting the medical, emotional, and spiritual care they need at the end of life. We sit in fear. Afraid to bring it up. Time passes. Meanwhile, our loved one fields emotions, questions, and the physical pain alone. Inside they may be asking:

What will it feel like? Will it be painful? Will my family be okay once I'm gone? What will happen to my pets? Who will take care of my belongings? Is God real? What will He think of me? Where will I be going? Will I get to say goodbye? Is there anything else we can do for my pain? Do they know that I hate to be alone?

....

While confronting death is scary, sometimes the ramifications of avoiding it are even scarier. When we refuse to accept death, this is what can happen:

We push elders when they really need rest.

We deny the elder a place to voice his or her fears.

We respond to symptoms with the wrong type of care.

We put our elder at risk of unnecessary suffering.

We deny the chance for an elder to share his or her end-of-life wishes.

We deny an older person the chance to have their wishes fulfilled.

We default to being an unequipped advocate because we don't know their wishes.

We don't feel the urgency to resolve past issues or to forgive.

Death occurs unexpectedly and it devastates us.

We miss the chance to say goodbye.

We feel regret.

We feel confused because we don't know how to handle the person's belongings or finances after they pass.

WHEN YOU ACCEPT DEATH

Over the years, as I've observed various family situations, I've noticed something: the best caregivers accept death. When you can accept death, you create space for beautiful things to happen. In accepting death, this is what we can do:

We can offer the elder a proper send-off.

We can celebrate their life and let them leave with pizzazz.

We are more convicted to apologize.

We have time to ask them what it means to finish life well.

We can offer them the medical support they need to be comfortable.

We can utilize hospice services earlier and position our elders for a better end.

We can acknowledge their fears about death (and there are many).

We can share deep conversation, allowing them to openly and honestly share how they are feeling (physically and emotionally) and thus allow professionals to offer them the best treatment for their symptoms.

We can call in friends and family to say goodbye.

We can share vulnerable, yet sacred, moments.

We have the gift of holding our loved one's hand.

We can say goodbye with a sense of peace, knowing
that we loved them until the end.

Aging is not all bad; for one, it serves as a nudge, a beloved
gift to cherish the weeks, days, hours, and minutes we have
with our elders. When we can accept death, we can grab the
remaining time we have left with someone and pack it with
precious words, humorous memories, comforting affection,
and unreserved love for our elder. This is the best way to handle the end.

ULTIMATELY, REMIND THEM

The sense I get from many adult children and grandchildren is
that as a parent or grandparent declines, they don't know what
to do. They feel ill-equipped.

*Is there something I should be doing now to prepare for later?
Do I need to have certain equipment on hand or certain forms filled
out? Will we be able to pay for eldercare? Will there come a time
when my loved one should live with us? What am I going to do
when they really need more help?*

It's true; there is no three-step process to completely prepare
you for caring for the older person. Aging is not a cookie-cutter
season of life, and it is impossible to research all the possibilities
or predict which trajectory your loved one's needs will take.

When Yeye, Mama, and Dad were nearing the end of their
lives, there were times we bounced back and forth in trying
to determine the best course of action. But was there ever re-

ally a "best?" Sometimes it felt like we were battling between chopped liver and lima beans (or the worst, mushrooms); neither option was satisfying. Neither option made us feel entirely at peace.

"I don't care if they live far away, the important thing is that they call and make me a part of their life by telling me things."

HELEN, 65

Then how can you be the best caregiver? How can you offer your grandparent, parent, or aging friend the best quality of life? In the midst of uncertainty, you should do what family and friends are made to do: love.

Because of my experience in the field, many friends have consulted me regarding an aging parent or grandparent. They feel anxious, not knowing what to do. But if there's anything I would recommend, whether your elder is healthy or whether they are nearing the end, it would be to remind your elder you love them.

"That's all?" you cry. "But there are physical needs and medical needs and appointments and equipment to think about."

Caregiving is full of unexpected turns. So while we heed the advice of the professionals and sometimes stumble to determine with the elder the best course of action, take heart; the medical issues may not be your forte, but they don't need to be. There's another job we need to assume, one that is reserved for you and me, one that we excel at.

We are the experts and most equipped to love our elders.
We know them best.
We know their needs.
We see them more than the professionals.

And so while we grow frantic and wonder what else we can do to offer the best quality of healthcare and life to our older friends, remember what your expertise is in and then put your efforts into that basket. Because while hired professionals and workers can be cheerful and loving and great company for our elders, what our elders want more than anything is to have family and friends near. Nothing beats close friends and, goodness, nothing beats family.

A NOBLE CALLING

When I reflect on my journey of living, loving, and serving the old, I laugh at how far I've come. From grumbling about why I had to grow up living with grandparents, to clocking in over a decade of experience working professionally in the field of aging, I now have this special place in my heart for older people.

Looking back, I've had quite a journey. One where every job of mine mirrored the needs of my family to their very end. From working in fitness, to assisted living and rehab, to hospice, I see that my professional experience allowed me to bless my elders in extremely meaningful ways. When Mama passed away, she was my last grandparent, and I thought for sure I had now completed my job of caring for the elderly.

But it was in the weeks after Mama's death, as my body rested, that my mind went into overdrive. And that's when I started to wonder.

What about the rest of the elderly? Who will speak for them when their health is failing? Who will sit with them and defend their pains? Do they have anyone who will be with them when they need a hand? Who in the world is going to be their voice?

In our prime younger years, we set off into the world motivated more than ever to make a difference. We sign up for the Peace Corps. We serve at soup kitchens. We travel overseas to care for orphans. We engage in political change.

Yet somehow in our effort to change the world, we have missed the fact that in addition to reducing poverty, pollution, crime, and evil in the world, in our very own neighborhood and family, there is life-changing work that can be done. In our midst is a generation full of rich stories, wisdom, knowledge, perseverance, personality, and love waiting to be discovered.

So it's time. I'm more convinced than ever that now is the time to use our hip, trendy, creative, energetic, innovative young selves to start a revolution in the way we honor our elders. So stand up. Salute. Refresh. Revitalize. Honor. Uplift. Respect. Comfort. Inspire. Encourage. Bless. And together, in small and big ways, let's remind the older generation of their value—wrinkles, white hair, and all. Time is ticking; so let's plan some memorable send-offs.

TAKE NOTES | *How to Throw a Proper Send-off*

Instead of a silent exit, every older adult needs a proper send-off. Here is a list of ideas on how to offer a loving and respectful send-off, particularly when you know someone is slowing down, getting tired, and nearing the end of their lives:

BE AN UNPAID VISITOR

Older adults need more unpaid visitors. When their main interaction is with hired help, it's understandable if they feel abandoned by their family. The greater the number of people (not paid to do so) who visit an older adult, the more the older adult is reminded how much they are loved. If you have an older friend who is not related, know that your visits can speak volumes; not only are you not paid, you also aren't related, and thus the older adult can see that you visit not out of obligation. Show up for no reason; this will mean so much to our older friends.

AVOID FAMILY DRAMA

Family relationships can get messy, but being civil for the sake of your parent's emotional well-being is a worthy cause. When an aging adult sees their family getting along, it not only brings them peace, it gives them great joy.

Even in peaceful families, however, conflict still arises. People have different opinions and this makes things complicated. If you and your siblings disagree, then don't ignore each other. Maybe take your disagreement somewhere else and out of the presence of the older parent.

Also, if you want to avoid family drama, the best thing you can do is to encourage the elder to talk about their wishes early (see Chapter 10). Doing so can be an antidote for family drama and can help resolve the differing opinions various family members have. As I mentioned earlier, when an aging parent has already communicated his wishes to the family, less conflict occurs.

LET THEM EAT ICE CREAM

Once we know someone has a limited amount of time left, we should focus less on prolonging their life and more on helping them enjoy every minute they have left. Rather than forcing an elder into a strict diet, a common practice at the end of life is to allow people to eat what they want, when they want it. Avoid the food struggle. And let them enjoy that ice cream.

HELP THEM NOT TO FEEL LIKE A BURDEN

If we want to bless an older adult, the best thing we can do for them is help them *not* to feel like a burden. Caring for an older person does require considerable time, effort, and sacrifice. Yet as we serve, rather than grumble over the workload, we need to remember how much courage it requires for the elder to ask for help and to have others assist them regularly with everyday tasks.

We must be intentional and consistent in reminding elders through nonverbal and verbal communication of their value. Because inside the mind of older adults is often the ingrained belief that as their bodies fade, so does their value.

Here are some truths older adults need to hear and be reminded of often. Use them generously. Say them repeatedly. Remind your elders of their value. Again. And again. Hearing is believed to be the last sense that goes when a person is dying, so speak these truths even up until the end:

> You are *so* special.
> I'm *so* glad to see you.
> I do it because I love you.
> I love you.

ONLY FOR
A LIMITED TIME

By the time Mama died at 102, I considered *and* claimed her as one of my best girlfriends. The kind that loves you so much, she'd even lend you her underwear. Really. My grandma's underwear came through for me. No, not *grandma* underwear, but literally *my* grandma's underwear rescued me after a four-day stay at the hospital.

I had a new infant in tow when, leaving the hospital, I knew my brand name underwear, whose stretch quality was once touted, was not going to cut it. Sadly, the hospital underwear wasn't going to cut it either. The doctor confirmed I was allergic to the hospital underwear. That was why my bottom was burning. Along with that, I had a fresh incision right below the waistline. I needed the softest, gentlest, most spacious and breathable underwear around. I needed space. And not to be demanding, but I needed it *soon*.

As we left the hospital and made our way over to my sister's house to pick up our other two kids, Kevin and I brainstormed my "underwear options." Going shopping for big underwear in my condition was not something I was up for; going shopping for big underwear was something Kevin was not up for either. Amazon Prime would not deliver soon enough. We parked in my sister's driveway, and as I dragged my unrecovered body and burning bottom up the front steps and into the house, I saw Mama sitting in her signature spot right by the door. I instantly shared my plight, and then remembered from all those years of helping wash her laundry that she had roomy and super elastic undies. Would she be okay if I borrowed some? Without hesitation, Mama shared what she had. I got the relief I desperately needed.

I don't know about you, but it's not every day you're blessed with a friend like that. Over thirty-five years, Mama became one of my best girlfriends, clearly the oldest one. Our relationship grew because of millions of minutes we spent together. As a child it's fairly easy to spend time with the old, yet as we hit adulthood the busyness of life often keeps us from making time for them. For me, my profession offered me many reminders that time was limited.

So as Mama got older and older, I was all the more determined to love her and spend as many minutes as I could with her. Anytime she needed someone to keep her company, I eagerly volunteered. When she landed in the hospital, I was happy to sit by her side. Yes, as she aged, she needed us to help. But I also realized I *wanted* to be with her.

As I think about my white-haired, wrinkled, beautiful

grandmother, I don't grieve as much as I beam over the special relationship I had with her. Though seemingly crummy in the beginning, I see that in actuality I was the one who was blessed. In living with and loving the old, without a doubt, my life was forever changed because of it. I am so grateful.

SOMETHING YOU SHOULD KNOW

In my professional career, I've had the luxury of working with skilled and caring colleagues who I could constantly tap into regarding my grandparents' and parents' health. From doctors to nurses to social workers to nursing home admissions counselors to administrators, the list goes on. When caring for any family member, it's important to understand that America's healthcare system is not only confusing, it is flawed. This is why we need to know how to navigate it. But there is truly so much to learn: from learning about how to navigate the hospital and doctor's office experience to understanding the services offered to older adults. If you are interested in learning some of the practical and precious jewels I've been given, visit www.isabeltom.com.

I'm cheering you on as you strive to love and honor the elders in your life.

ACKNOWLEDGMENTS

There are many people to thank for making this book happen. Can I get a microphone, please?

Mom and Dad, you were the first ones to show me how to value the elderly. I saw your sweat, tears, energy, and hearts poured into loving Mama and Yeye through even the hard times. Because of your commitment, you blessed me with the chance to live with my grandparents. What you did evolved into this book, one that I believe will bless many.

Mom, thank you for being my agent and promoting this book before I even finished it. Thank you for not expecting me to be a straight-A student, but for nurturing the unique gifts, skills, and abilities God has given me. Thank you for loving me through your prayer. You are the ultimate example of fun and adventure later in life. I aspire to be like that one day.

Jo and Priscilla, I'm spoiled to have sisters like you. Thank you for cheering me on every step of the process.

Jo and Jason, thank you for letting an annoying little sister live with you for so many years. You sacrificed the freedom of being young to bless Mama and Yeye, and if not for you both, an important part of this story would not have happened.

Priscilla and Albert, thank you for praying over my family and my writing and for being some of our best buddies to hang out with.

Julia, Jonathan, Josiah, Jubilee, Charis, and Ally, I love you guys and have so much fun being your aunt.

To my mother-in-law, Mary, thank you for being my other agent. I am blessed beyond measure by your enthusiasm, generosity, and unconditional support. EJ, I'm blessed to have a kind brother-in-law like you.

To the entire Moody team, I give you a standing ovation. Judy, I was hoping I would get this book contract, simply because I wanted to work with you. You exude the love of Christ and have treated me better than a client, but like a daughter through your caring spirit. To Amanda, you took the words out of this mommy brain and magically made sense of them; thank you for having patience with a first-timer like me. A special thanks also to Erik, Ashley, Connor, Kelsey, Siri, and everyone on the amazing marketing, design, and proofreading teams for the behind-the-scenes work you have done to spread the message of this book and help make it shine. If I worked in your office, I would be coming by often to thank you and the rest of the Moody team profusely.

To Compel Training, thank you for teaching me how to use words to speak life into others. I learned everything I needed to know about publishing and writing through your program.

To the mentors and colleagues I had at Erickson Living/

Riderwood, you are some of the most fun and caring professionals around. I consider it an honor to have learned from and served with you.

To my friends and former colleagues at Montgomery Hospice, thank you for teaching me so much and for showing me how to value people until the very end and for walking me through the hardest losses. Your skill and compassion will not be forgotten.

To those I interviewed for this book, thank you for honestly sharing your thoughts with me. Your insight added the perfect touch to this book and I know it will speak to many.

To Amanda Leung, Maria Mapa Kim, Nicole Christenson, Beza Gebrehana, Esther Cho, Irene Park, Tiffany Fong, Pearl Mak, Kristie Loo, Sally Roberts, Joseph Sit, Winyan SooHoo, Brigit Sullivan, Mary Wassmann, and all those who provided me with their feedback throughout the writing process. Thank you for helping me perfect the message of this book.

To Jane Daly and Jennifer FitzPatrick, thank you for taking the time to support me as a writer and encouraging me to get to this point.

To Dorothy, thank you for being the ultimate moral support and for driving hours with me to pitch this book. You're one of a kind. Thank you for cheering me on.

To Lins, you were one of my best sounding boards and the first friend I trusted to read my work. I am so blessed to have a friend like you.

To my friends, aunties, prayer warriors, and other cheerleaders, I can't find any vocabulary word to describe how grateful I am for you. Your support means so much.

To Maddie, Sam, and Ben, thank you for distracting me with your cute faces, hugs, laughs, handcrafted notes, recommended edits and titles as I wrote this book. You are God's grace in my life and being your mommy is an honor. I love you!

To Kevin, you of all people helped make this into a book. Thank you for graciously walking this journey with me, playing with the kids so I could write, and believing in me. Our late-night snack chats were the beginning of most of my ideas. Thank you for killing spiders in the basement and bringing me water and food, so I could write and write and write. You deserve a medal, and I hope to get to hear your jokes and see your handsome face for decades to come. Love.

To Jesus Christ my Lord and Savior, thank You for working a beautiful story out of my life even when I didn't know it. Even when I grumbled. You are worthy of all my praise. Thank You for using me to speak life into a whole generation; I could not be more honored.

NOTES

CHAPTER 1: THAT WASN'T A WHITE HAIR, WAS IT?

1. "Proposed working definition of an older person in Africa for the MDS Project," World Health Organization, 2002, https://www.who.int/healthinfo/survey/ageingdefnolder/en/.
2. "QuickFacts," U.S. Census Bureau, taken from July 1, 2018 estimates, https://www.census.gov/quickfacts/fact/table/US/AGE775218#AGE775218.
3. "A Profile of Older Americans: 2017," Administration on Aging (AoA), Administration for Community Living, U.S. Department of Health and Human Services, April 2018, https://acl.gov/sites/default/files/Aging%20and%20Disability%20in%20America/2017OlderAmericansProfile.pdf.

CHAPTER 2: I'VE GOT TIME FOR YOU

1. Andy Molinksy and Sheila Pisman, "The Biggest Hurdles Recent Graduates Face Entering the Workforce," *Harvard Business Review*, April 11, 2019, https://hbr.org/2019/04/the-biggest-hurdles-recent-graduates-face-entering-the-workforce.
2. "How Memory Loss Happens: Understanding Alzheimer's," *Aging Care*, accessed September 2, 2019, https://www.agingcare.com/articles/memory-loss-in-alzheimers-148992.htm.

CHAPTER 4: REAL-LIFE ENCOUNTERS

1. Personal Interview, John Erickson, March 8, 2019.

CHAPTER 5: AN UNTAPPED RESOURCE

1. Lexico, s.v. "Wisdom," https://www.lexico.com/en/definition/wisdom.

CHAPTER 6: STEP UP

1. "Nursing Home Care," Centers for Disease Control and Prevention, last reviewed March 11, 2016, https://www.cdc.gov/nchs/fastats/nursing-home-care.htm.
2. "She had never seen the ocean. Now, with her grandson, she's seen 29 national parks," WJLA, published August 6, 2019, https://wjla.com/news/local/grandson-grandmother-national-parks-adventure.
3. Gary Chapman, *The 5 Love Languages* (Chicago: Northfield Publishing, 2015), 75–86.
4. Jennifer L. FitzPatrick, *Cruising through Caregiving* (Austin, TX: Greenleaf Book Group Press, 2016), 47.
5. Ibid., 47–48.
6. Robert Perske, "The Dignity of Risk and the Mentally Retarded," *Mental Retardation* 10, no. 1 (1972): 24–27, http://www.robertperske.com/Articles.html.
7. "Caring Relationships: The Heart of Early Brain Development," National Association for the Education of Young Children, May 2017, https://www.naeyc.org/resources/pubs/yc/may2017/caring-relationships-heart-early-brain-development.
8. "What Every Child Needs for Good Mental Health," Mental Health America, revised February 2000, https://www.mentalhealthamerica.net/every-child-needs.
9. Debbie Barr, Edward G. Shaw, and Gary Chapman, *Keeping Love Alive as Memories Fade* (Chicago: Northfield, 2016), 123.

CHAPTER 7: WHEN YOU'VE GOT A "LEMON"

1. "Why Sleep Deprivation Is Torture," *Psychology Today*, December 15, 2014, https://www.psychologytoday.com/us/blog/dreaming-in-the-digital-age/201412/why-sleep-deprivation-is-torture.

2. Keisuke Suzuki, Masayuki Miyamoto, and Koichi Hirata, "Sleep Disorders in the Elderly," *Journal of General and Family Medicine* (2017), 61–71, https://onlinelibrary.wiley.com/doi/full/10.1002/jgf2.27.

3. Email exchange with Nicole Christenson, August 5, 2019.

4. Institute of Medicine (US) Committee on Advancing Pain Research, Care, and Education, *Relieving Pain in America: A Blueprint for Transforming Prevention, Care, Education, and Research* (Washington DC: National Academies Press, 2011), https://www.ncbi.nlm.nih.gov/pubmed/22553896.

5. Ibid.

6. "The Power of Kisses," Greater Good Science Center at UC Berkeley, July 28, 2010, https://greatergood.berkeley.edu/article/item/the_power_of_kisses.

7. Grace Lebow and Barbara Kane, *Coping With Your Difficult Older Parent: A Guide for Stressed-Out Children* (New York: Quill, 1999), 60.

CHAPTER 8: OLD IS HEALTHY

1. Summer Allen, "The Science of Gratitude," John Templeton Foundation, Greater Good Science Center at UC Berkeley, May 2018, 4, https://ggsc.berkeley.edu/images/uploads/GGSC-JTF_White_Paper-Gratitude-FINAL.pdf.

2. Summer Allen, "The Science of Gratitude," John Templeton Foundation, Greater Good Science Center at UC Berkeley, May 2018, 2, 28, https://ggsc.berkeley.edu/images/uploads/GGSC-JTF_White_Paper-Gratitude-FINAL.pdf.

3. Paul J. Mills, Laura Redwine, Kathleen Wilson, Meredith A. Pung, Kelly Chinh, Barry H. Greenberg, Ottar Lunde, Alan Maisel, Ajit Raisinghani, Alex Wood, Deepak Chopra, "The Role of Gratitude in Spiritual Well-Being in Asymptomatic Heart Failure Patients," *Spirituality in Clinical Practice* 2, no. 1 (2015): 5–17, http://dx.doi.org/10.1037/scp0000050.

4. "Health and Well-Being Benefits of Plants," Ellison Chair in International Floriculture, https://ellisonchair.tamu.edu/health-and-well-being-benefits-of-plants/#.WfMlOGiPLif.

CHAPTER 9: BUILDING A VILLAGE

1. "Caregiver Health," Family Caregiver Alliance, published 2006, https://www.caregiver.org/caregiver-health.
2. Ibid.
3. Gary Chapman, *The 5 Love Languages: The Secret to Love That Lasts* (Chicago: Northfield, 2015).
4. Personal Interview, John Erickson, March 8, 2019.
5. Debbie Barr, Edward Shaw, and Gary Chapman, *Keeping Love Alive as Memories Fade* (Chicago: Northfield, 2016), 92.

CHAPTER 10: TAKE ADVANTAGE OF THE SWEET SPOT

1. Blythe Daniel and Helen McIntosh, *Mended: Restoring the Hearts of Mothers and Daughters* (Eugene, OR: Harvest House Publishers, 2019), 27.
2. Personal Interview with Mary Wassmann, RN, CHPN, and Sally Roberts, RN, CHPN, June 4, 2019.
3. Personal Interview with Kip Ingram at Montgomery Hospice, Spring 2019.
4. Shahid Aziz, *Courageous Conversations on Dying: The Gift of Palliative Care* (Scotts Valley, CA: CreateSpace Independent Publishing Platform, 2018), 11.
5. Ira Byock, *The Four Things That Matter Most* (New York: Atria Books, 2014), 4.
6. Ibid., 3.
7. "Mortality in the United States, 2017" Centers for Disease Control and Prevention, NCHS Data Brief No. 328, November 2018, https://www.cdc.gov/nchs/products/databriefs/db328.htm.
8. Byock, *The Four Things That Matter Most*, 5.

CHAPTER 11: HER SITTING YEARS

1. Loren Shook and Stephen Winner, *The Silverado Story: A Memory-Care Culture Where Love Is Greater than Fear* (Irvine, CA: AJC Press, 2010), 12.

2. "The 2019 Florida Statutes," Official Internet Site of the Florida Legislature, 2019, http://www.leg.state.fl.us/statutes/index.cfm? App_mode=Display_Statute&URL=0400-0499/0400/Sections/ 0400.23.html.

3. "Statistics and Data," National Center on Elder Abuse, https:// ncea.acl.gov/About-Us/What-We-Do/Research/Statistics-and-Data.aspx#ltc.

4. Ibid.

WHY DO WE ACT LIKE THERE IS AN AGE RESTRICTION ON SPIRITUAL GROWTH?

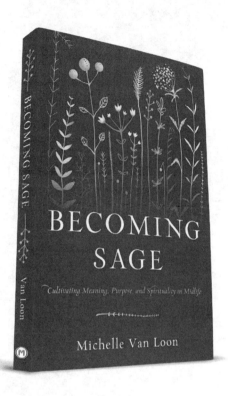

Churches today often focus their resources on the early stages of discipleship. While this is important, the spiritual growth of those in the second half of life must not be neglected. Through *Becoming Sage*, reimagine the challenges of midlife as an opportunity for revitalized growth in Christ.

978-0-8024-1944-6